HOW TO ACQUIRE MONEY

PETER-OYEBOBOLA

authorHOUSE®

AuthorHouse™ UK Ltd.
500 Avebury Boulevard
Central Milton Keynes, MK9 2BE
www.authorhouse.co.uk
Phone: 08001974150

First published by AuthorHouse 8/31/2011

ISBN: 978-1-4567-7234-5 (sc)

y to everyone reading this book thanks for purchasing and for
ssing, I pray this book will transform your life and take you to
vel.

<u>DEDICATIONS</u>

is dedicated to the fellows who are hungry for the true riches. For
ple who are faithful supporters of good works and contributing a
(Financially) to any one whom God send on their way- YOUR
AS COME congratulation this is your book.

And fina
been a bl
another

ACKNOWLEGI

This book is powerful revelation from abo
other teaching derived from my Mentors, I
Teachers best known in the body of Christ

The journey of a life time will not be conc
story of the helpers of destiny who have cont
Either known or unknown individual they
endless supports and here are just a few who

Firstly I will forever be grateful to the Almi
of the hidden treasures" that gives power to
all teachers who gave all the wisdom inside

My mother Chief Elisabeth Folake - Oyebo
her 100 years of age, for your angelic educa
from my birth even though you are illiterate

To the late archbishop Benson Idahosa, I w
wealth transfer anointing oil place upon my
one of his crusade in London.

Special thanks to the following people, sister
for the transcript) Venorila (USA) Lious (UK
the proof reading of this book. Also the staff
for your professionalism and final touch on

To the members and followers of ICCC/PRA
opportunity to develop, share the whole idea
in our relationship over the years. Thanks fo

To my darling wife the queen of my heart
Thanks for your love and supports.

This boo
those pec
faith seec
TIME H

CHAPTERS

INTRODUCTION

Behind every closed door, something is hidden. Likewise, every open door carries a deeper significance. If you've seen a tree planted in the middle of the road, it must surely contain significant history. As the proverb goes, there is no smoke without fire. In every book written, there is always a motivation in the mind of the author - whether this is good or bad.

Many people have turned to various wicked means of acquiring wealth. In the process of making money, they have tried all kinds of things, such as selling harmful medications and trafficking illegal drugs across the Atlantic Ocean. Some have joined occults, visiting various fetish doctors who perform rituals for the sake of making money. King Solomon is recorded as the wealthiest man in the history of the world. Despite all of his wealth and riches, he wrote the following words: ***"Vanity, all is vanity"***.

WHY I WROTE THIS BOOK

Because of the lure of money, many youths are living in the fast lane killing and robbing innocent citizens at gun point, all for the sake of acquiring more money. Shamefully enough, some even sell their own children into sex slavery, murder their partners to benefit from their life insurance and many other similar unbelievable stories.

The Bible states: ***But understand this that in the last days there will come times of difficulty. 2 For people will be lovers of self, lovers of money, proud, arrogant, abusive, disobedient to their parents, ungrateful, unholy, 3 heartless, unappeasable, slanderous, without self-control, brutal, not loving good, 4 treacherous, reckless, swollen with conceit, lovers of pleasure rather than lovers of God. (2Timothy 3:1-4)***

Today, the situation is getting worse, with the arrival of the latest technologies such as the internet. People don't have to travel miles before they can commit atrocity. Terrorist acts are spreading like cancer and people are not afraid to take somebody's life for the sake of money.

The love of money is the root of all evil and the lack of money is a prevalent concern.

I could have called this book "The Secret of Success". However, many people including children, understand the meaning of money more than success and when people are asked about what it means to be successful, many will judge it based on the money value (though success is not limited to money).

The lure of money has captivated the minds of people to the extent that the concept of God has now become like that of a third class citizen. Many, including church goers who call themselves Christians, seem to have no regard for the following scripture: *But seek first his kingdom and his righteousness, and all these things will be given to you as well.* **(Matthew 6:33).**

It's as if they have turned it around and they focus more on the money, rather than the Kingdom of God and his righteousness. Do you say this is not true? If you think this statement is not right, please observe people's actions around you. People talk more about money and the devil's power than God's power in action.

LEARN THE SECRET

The primary purpose of the church is to teach society how to live a better life and to guide the hearts of people back to God and should lead a balanced life. I strongly believe in being taught the real truth about how to make money the right way and to understand the will of God concerning the issue of money. Everything in life belongs to God the creator of heaven and earth; he owns it all. *"The thousand cattle on the hill belong to me"*

Another reason why I wrote this book is to provide a learning source for people so that instead of them learning from an ungodly generation, this book which is a revelation from God, can teach people how to be free from financial burdens, crossing from the bondage of poverty into the abundant blessings of God.

Most of the information in this book is not just based on personal ideas but rather they are a deep revelation from the Almighty Father of Light.

The promises of God still remain unchangeable *Deut.29:29* says

"The secret things belong to God and such a revelation is for us and our children."

You might have read many books relating to secrets that are actually based on fact. Even after you've tried everything described in those books, you are yet to see the result and some of you have been discouraged by most of the information shared by many authors. For your information, *the Word of God is not all about fact but based on the solid truth*. The truth you know will determine how far you can go.

THE PROBLEM OF LIFE

There are three main problems in life. Namely, Pride of life, the Lust of the flesh and the Lust of the eyes. In other words you can also translate this statement into something more understandable: Position, Women and Money. Rather than addressing these issues, most people beat about the bush. For example, instead of using the word sex, they say they sleep together which has been so confusing and if you ever say you sleep with your sister, someone is thinking something is not right with that picture. What a confusing world! The subject of money in the church has been a no-go zone because of the complication and the misinterpretation among the people. Instead of people asking God in prayer for money, they'd rather pray for God's blessing. Meanwhile, to be blessed also means to have more money to accomplish your assignment.

Money may not be all things but money answers all things!

MY HEARTY APPRECIATION

Thanks to the many authors who have written on the subject of money in one way or another, based on their life experiences. I will forever be grateful for their contributions. In my own case, I wrote this book based on a revelation from God and my life experience, including some of the knowledge that I have gathered from many books that I have read in my life.

The Bible contains all of the information that will lead to our success. My prayer and advice is that the Holy Spirit will guide you into all truth, grant you the utterance to access and make use of all information available inside this book, which I believe will work for you. Please don't just read this book once, read it at all times for a better result and I will see you on the other side of success.

MY PRAYER:

I pray for everyone reading this book that, the Lord will open your heart of understanding to see far beyond any limitations, grant you wisdom to apply every principal thought inside this God given revelation of a book and the mind to retain all of the information enclosed within its pages.

I destroy every mind-set of poverty that already lies within the mind. The Bible says while men were sleeping, the enemy came. Every sleeping object I rebuke; I pray that your brain will be more active so that your life can become better with great success. I activate every seed of knowledge and wisdom in your life to come forth and bear your fruit in your season. Everything you put your hand to, from now on, shall prosper in the mighty name of Jesus Christ, Amen.

CHAPTER ONE
DEALING WITH THE GRASS ROOTS

Poverty cannot deprive us of many consolations. It cannot rob us of the affection we have for each other, or degrade us in our own opinion, or in that of any person, whose opinion we ought to value.
Ann Radcliffe

The foundation of the universe was the beginning of humanity; no smoke without fire. As you all know, a thousand mile journey starts with one step. Every house built started from the foundation. The history of money originated from addressing the issue of poverty. For every tree to stand upright, the root must be dealt with properly.

The story of making money will not be good enough if the poverty root is not dealt with. Firstly, as you know, no baby was ever born without the true story of a parent. A millionaire is not just born, rather a millionaire is made and this is because they deal brutally with the root of poverty. Just like the iron that went through the hot fire and came out refined, a successful person has a little story to tell about his riches. Every time you ask a successful man a question; he has a little story to tell about his journey to the new place of arrival. But, you can also learn a great deal of lessons from a poor person. I want to share with you what it means to be poor.

Poverty is an issue that not everyone finds interesting to study and a book about poverty or failure has never been easy to find at the bookshop. But the fact remains that on the average, many of the world's population live in absolute poverty. Let's take a look at something similar in the Bible.

"The wife of a man from the company of the prophets cried out to Elisha, "Your servant my husband is dead, and you know that he revered the LORD. But now his creditor is coming to take my two boys as his slaves." 2 Elisha replied to her, "How can I help you? Tell me, what do you have in your house?" "Your servant has nothing there at all," she said, "except a little oil." 3 Elisha said "Go around and ask

all your neighbors for empty jars. Don't ask for just a few. 4 Then, go and shut the door behind you and your sons. Pour oil into all the jars, and as each is filled, put it to one side." 5 She left him and afterward shut the door behind her and her sons. They brought the jars to her and she kept pouring. 6 When all the jars were full, she said to her son, "Bring me another one." But he replied, "There is not a jar left." Then the oil stopped flowing. 7 She went and told the man of God, and he said, "Go, sell the oil and pay your debts. You and your sons can live on what is left." 2KINGS 4:1-7

POVERTY HAS NO BOUNADRIES

In my mindset as an African-born black man, I was made to understand that my race is the poorest in the whole universe and we are living under the label of 'Third World'. However, to my wildest imagination, when I arrived in Europe, I saw some of the greatest levels of poverty among white people. I now understand that poverty is a general disease which needs to be dealt with throughout the entire human race, irrespective of color, race, or gender.

The opposite of money is lack of it which can also be called Poverty or a state of being poor. When you are poor, you cannot meet your needs. When you are poor, you cannot afford to eat food regularly . When you are poor, society will look down on you and say nothing good comes out of you. ***Poverty comes as a result of little mistakes; it is not a desire, but an act of foolishness.*** Nobody wants to be poor. Let's face the reality of life and understand here at this point, there is nothing you can do; some people will remain poor until they die. "I refuse poverty". I can identify people's poverty mentality depending on how they speak to me because there is an attitude towards riches and there's also an attitude towards poverty.

Nobody on this earth desires to be poor. Nobody ever wakes up early in the morning and plans to live the rest of their life in poverty. For your information, everyone wants to be rich or debt- free in life. Let me ask you a question: Is everybody rich? Do you think everybody out there has sufficient cash in their bank account or is able to make ends meet?

Most people are broke and shattered; their lives are totally dependent on others for the ability to afford ordinary daily food. What a rat race lifestyle! No wonder the Holy book says "The lender rules over the borrower".

PARENTAL INFLUENCE

The majority of people borrow the idea of poverty from their parents.

Because a poverty mentality starts from wrong teachings such as you need to work hard in order to be rich, or study and acquire a lot of degrees in the university if you really want to be rich. A great deal of pressure is on society. To be blunt, what I find is that these are all lies from the devil and I will take you through them in greater detail in the 'Lies of Money' in Chapter 3 of this book.

I recommend a book which had blessed my life titled *RICH DAD, POOR DAD*, by ROBERT T. KIYOSAKI. This book will give you the insight to what your parents have implanted to your life without even knowing it. . Remember, what you hear will affect your thinking and your thinking will affect your sight which leads to what proceeds out of your mouth. Whatever you say, will determine how you live your life.

Anybody who is poor, is poor because he or she made mistakes somewhere in life; that's why everybody has a story to tell. A rich man however, does not have an excuse for failure because he has attained success. Have you ever wondered, while running a race on the field, how the winners break the record? Their reply will be very simple and brief, saying all glory to God! They will only let you know that their success is because they've practiced more often, but on the other hand, if you ask a failure, they will answer with twenty million and ten thousand excuses just to explain to you what actually led to the failure. Life may be full of excuses. Please remember there is no excuse for failure, so never attempt to be a failure. Nobody wants to read a failure's story, but a successful man's book will put more food on his table and create a better future for the next generation.

"A good man will leave an inheritance for his fourth generation."
May God make you great and able to overcome every poverty in life.

HOW TO CROSS THE BRIDGE

The bridge between the rich and the poor in our society is the 'WISDOM PRINCIPLE'. One is able to apply wisdom and the other one isn't. Let me tell you, many people started a business like you did, but why did they fold up? Many people went to the same university as you, but why are they still shattered and broke? Many people are married like you, why did they get a divorce? The answer to all these questions is in "Wisdom"

The bible says in the book of proverbs: *"Wisdom is the principle thing. With all thy getting, get understanding"*.

Acquire wisdom and refuse foolishness because foolishness will take you nowhere. When you see somebody who has failed or is successful there is one key. When you see someone who acts or is not acting- there is one key. For one who is fast or one who is slow- one key and the key is called "WISDOM". Every vision or inspiration you got from God can only become reality as long as wisdom is in operation, when you find wisdom you find life. I will explain more about this in Chapter 5.

GREAT IDEAS DEMAND EXCELLENT REWARD

Those who make money in our society nowadays will admit that their riches are as a result of the efforts of others, people who got the original idea, but have little understanding on how to implement such vision. They somehow took the opportunity and made use of it because of the wisdom on their side.

One of the richest men on Earth, Bill Gates, made use of the wisdom principles. The first thing he did when he got the idea of establishing Microsoft was to license it to himself. He then instructed every intelligent student studying computing, that upon discovering any new software programme or any other computer usage programme, and it should be written and legalized in his own name. Let me tell you, Bill Gates is not the one who wrote Microsoft Word. He's not the one who discovered your voicemail, word processor, Window Media etc. but because he used his own wisdom and ideas together, he is credited with the discovery. Even until this day, you will not have heard of anyone who has written all those programs on your computer, but everything is owned by Windows, licensed and incorporated to Bill Gates. What a great idea, Wisdom in operation. I see you crossing from foolishness into wisdom and making use of the wisdom that will lead you to a greater level in life! Just believe in yourself, hold on to what is in your mind, and in due season it will happen, if you never give up.

THE DANGER OF POVERTY

Poverty is very bad because if care is not taken, a believer can even deny the Almighty God in an attempt to avoid it. Poverty is so bad that you can deny your father or mother. May God elevate you from poverty. You are serving a big God, but sometimes people make a big God to be a small God. You say 'NO' I can't deny God, but that's what kept you from church meetings most of the time. Your employer gave you a common overtime at work and you denied your service to God. King Solomon cried unto God in ***Pro.30:8*** saying:*"Give me no riches or poverty that will make me deny you"*

Some married couples cheat on their spouse because of poverty. Children will deny their parents by dishonoring them. Friends or relatives will close their doors and pretend they do not know you. My brethren, poverty is a game of shame, and only those who play the game know the shame.

If you have never been poor in your life, you may not understand what I am talking about, but I want you to know that poverty is real. Those who are poor or who have been poor will give a thumbs up and accept that I am stating the truth. I pray you will not be poor in life.

THE FLY THAT TASTES LIKE A SHRIMP

Let me share a story of a pastor friend who God has elevated now.

While he was going through a poverty-stricken season in his life, an incident happened. He was staying with a friend in a local remote area and life became so tough that there was no good food to eat or good water to drink. Both of them went through the poverty of life.

One day, luckily enough, somebody gave them food to eat. Unfortunately, a big fly entered the food. Out of ignorance, my pastor friend thought it was meat, (as the fly looked like a big piece of shrimp) only to discover it was a fly. What else could he do? It was the only meal available for the day. Without the hope of more food, of course they continued to eat the rest of the food with gladness of their hearts. Whoa! Disgusting! Is it not?

I REFUSE TO BE POOR

Poverty will deny you of life's benefits and separates you from friends and relatives.

Prov.19:4. *Wealth brings many friends, but a poor man's friends desert him.*

A rich man has many friends, but who knows a poor man or wants to associate with poor people? There are benefits in life available to the fortunate ones. Just imagine flying in an air craft. Some people are in first class; their nails are being treated, because they have VIP tickets to go on first class. Whereas some of you when you want to travel, you only look for the cheapest hotel; buy your ticket many days in advance to get it cheaper. A poor man says he has an idea; the idea will definitely die with him if care is not taken. After all, what can an idea produce when there is no money to implement it?

May God give you money to go about all the ideas in your heart.

NO EXCUSE FOR FAILURE

To be poor means you are underprivileged which also mean failure. You failed yourself, the government, your family, society and everybody, including your own children. There is no excuse for failure, when you fail, you have failed. Even when you wish to talk, no one listens. No one wants to know the fact that your father was poor, that's why you couldn't make it. Nobody wants to know the reason why you cannot secure a well paid job is due to your lack of education. No excuse you come up with will be acceptable from the perspective of man in this generation. People can only sympathize with you for a while. That is all! So please never join a pity party wagon. A poor man may say 'I don't like money.' It's not that he doesn't like it, but there's no way for him to get it.

Poverty is a matter of the mind. **Your thinking priority will determine your living mentality**. The bible says "as a man thinks in his heart so is he". How do you know if you are poor? The way you speak or react to matter of needs either yourself or that of others will definitely show how poor you are. When you are talking to people and your speech gets them irritated, you better acknowledge this is another symptom of lack. Some people are so poor that even the poor call them poor. They are poor in their relationship; poor in their health, poor financially, psychologically, in fact they are poor in all area of life. When you are poor, even if you are given a million, you will definitely mess it up. Do you know that it is recorded that among those who won the lottery, 90% will go back poor and shattered?

POVERTY IS A MATTER OF THE MIND

If you give the sum of £2000 to someone with a poverty stricken mentality, they only need 24 hrs to lavish the money and before the closing of the day, there is possibility that they will return back telling you the excuse surrounding the money; and if care is not taken, the person can even tell you they need more money to settle the problems that resulted from the money you gave them.

Poverty is a matter of the mind, that's why, the book of **Romans.12:2** says *"And do not be conformed to this world, but be transformed by* *the renewing of your mind, that you may prove what is that good and acceptable and perfect will of God"*

Some people want to be rich, but what do they need money for. This is why some people, despite the fact of their desperation, make money only to return to being even more broken than before and live in absolutely poverty.

Poverty is like a virus, if not properly treated, it could affect a whole generation even up to the next generation. Ask your mother, why is she poor, she will tell you because her grandmother was poor. So, the story continues. The bible says "this story shall no longer be heard in the land of Israel that a mother eats a grape and the daughter's mouth is sour" This simply means the poverty of a parent will not necessary affect their own children. In other words, if your mother is poor you may not be affected as long as you position yourself.

CUTTING OFF THE TAPE

Your father or mother made the mistake, why are you paying for it? Your mother left your father because he was poor and now you say I don't care if my husband leaves me, we are used to that in our family. Do you know what you are saying? you'd better stand your ground. We have to cut the flow of poverty. If you have friends or close relatives who are poor, they will bother you and bug your life. They will pick up the phone to call you as early as 5am just to seek your financial support. I refuse that you carry over your parent's poverty, it is better to gain more intelligence by working smartly and provide for your future. The bible says a good man leaves an inheritance for his children's children.

THOSE WHO BEG HAVE A CHOICE

I have one philosophy in my life; I would rather teach people the principle of making money or how to catch fish rather than giving them money. Why? If I give you money instead of bait, you will come back to beg for fish. That's why if you come to me to borrow money, you are in the wrong place. I will give you the idea of how to make that money.

Poverty is a curse and the only way out of it is to break out of it because poverty is not something anybody plans for. Poverty loves simple people because if you are simple, poverty will be a tenant, sleep and wake up with you, rob you of your wife, family and rob you of your life's benefit because you are poor and foolish.

Psalm.66:12 says "*You have caused men to ride over our heads; we went through fire and through water; But you brought us out to rich fulfillment.*"

In simple language, we have gone through poverty, lack of food, economic crisis, lack of education, immigration control, and all sort of circumstances. We have gone through all these but you brought us out into a place of success.

NEVER MISS THE TRAIN

Can I tell you the irony of life? If you let all the revelation in this book go empty handed, it would be a big shame and I'd wonder how you can get it over again. In other words, please kindly digest all the information and make use of the best as quickly as you can. I pray that God will grant you the understanding to do the right thing in life and be successful by the grace of God, but remember you have a part to play. There shall be no lack.

God does not benefit from anyone being a failure; he delights in our riches. Some people say it does not matter if I die poor, I will go to heaven. You are joking! The good part of life is to make use of the best here on earth by enjoying all the benefit God provided for us on Earth and when we get to heaven, we still enjoy ourselves.

BASIC THINGS THAT LEAD TO POVERTY

Many things usually lead to poverty and the more you recognize the main cause of this problem the better and easier life will become. I do not in any way claim that everything I listed in these pages are the only reason behind poverty, rather the more you observe carefully, the quicker you get out of poverty. Remember: there is no ignorance before the law and if a principle once worked, it will work again. After all, people exchange their ignorance which makes them in the pursuit to acquire more money.

1. LOVER OF PLEASURE.

"*He who loves pleasure will be a poor man; He who loves wine and oil will not be rich Prov.21:17*

Some people live a fantasy life and this will lead to poverty. Whatever you have, be contented. Cutting your colt according to your size is a secret of life - don't do more than you are supposed to do. Don't show off to people. Don't get, hire or purchase a car when you don't earn enough money to pay for the petrol. Don't live in a house you cannot afford to pay the rent. Many people in the process of impressing another person live a fantasy lifestyle; chasing after the wind. They live above their income, associating themselves with high class people. They party all night long, every single day of life, buying the most expensive clothes.

Never pretend as if you don't know what I am talking about. Some of them live in our neighborhood.

In today's society, the tradition of carrying cash in our pocket is merely a disappearing history. Most banks, especially in Europe, now offer people credit cards with available cash in excess of their salaries and after spending unnecessarily, buying what is not needed, people are back into the corner leading to depression and frustration.

LEARN FROM MY PERSONAL STORY.

I remember some time ago in 2004, when we newly started our ministry base in North London, things were tough financially. The reason being, as pastor, our main calling is to reach the people on the street, such as prostitutes, drug addicts etc. and because of this, my wife and I were the ones responsible for all the expenses in the ministry. To add insult to injury, we decided to change our business from a hairdressing salon to a care agency, which crashed our financial system from hero to zero.

Things fell apart. We went through fire and instead of finding a way out, we chose to go to the way of credit cards. Trust me; every credit available at our hand became a savior. We paid for everything we shouldn't't have paid for and bought what we ought not to have bought in the first place. We entered deeper into debt. We went from broke to poverty. To worsen the situation, fear dominated our life because we lived a fake life using other people's money to pay for our lifestyle. Eventually, we were unable to settle the credit cards' debt. Higher interest were added which almost cost us our life if not for God the almighty who intervened.

There are people who borrow money just to travel or go on vacation. Some even use credit cards to do silly things in life and by the time they have to pay back, they have to pay with their blood and some even lose their life and dreams.

2. LAZINESS

"The lazy man will not plough because of winter; He will beg during harvest and have nothing. **Prov.20:4**

The opposite of laziness is hard work. Any man who is diligent in whatever he does, will dine with noble people. A lazy man will stand with mere men who eat the bread of sorrow. A lazy person finds it difficult to wake up early in the morning which is a start of the day. Everything becomes too tiring and uncomfortable. If you are lazy, you are useless because people want to associate with others who are capable enough to take them to another level- which is far away from a lazy fellow.

In the society, today everything is fast and furious. I call it the generation of the flying eagles. Nobody likes to waste time because time is money. A lazy person will stop you from getting to the finish line- not because they cannot run, but because they find it difficult to start the race.

A wife was once asked "what is the secret behind your working so hard". She replied 'I am married to a lazy man who finds it impossible to do anything since we became husband and wife. And to crown the injury with insult, my husband is a domineering man who just sits in front of the television every single day, switching from one station to another, demanding food, drink and all the nicest things in life. Immediately when the doctor told me I was pregnant with a baby boy, I quickly had to speak sense to myself, get out there, and stand for the good of my family; because I will never let my boy follow the footsteps of his lazy father. He is good for nothing.'

USE YOUR BRAIN NOT YOUR HEAD

When you are lazy, you are good for nothing. Life is not for the lazy, but for the strong people. Where a strong man survives, a lazy fellow will crash like a wicked man who falls and nobody helps him to get up. No matter what may be your excuse, never be lazy because if you do, it will be impossible to acquire money or any life achievements. Although not everybody is born with 5-star strength, as long as there is breath in you, always try to do something. Whether little, or just a step out, the more you try, the better you become and eventually master the situation.

Successful people on earth hate to be idle because they never love to eat the bread of idleness; that is why they develop life styles which make them stand out from the crowd and that is why today they are where they dreamed to be. You also can get there only if you avoid laziness. Don't be lazy. Be a working person. Your brain must be working. Laziness is a criminal offense. If you are lazy, you have a problem -period.

3. SLEEPING TOO MUCH

Do not loves sleep, lest you come to poverty; Open your eyes, and you will be satisfied with bread. Proverbs 20:13

When people sleep then wake up, the body becomes refreshed. Without adequate sleep, the body organs will not function properly. Sleep is God's gift to humankind and sleep is good. Everybody desires to sleep.

The point is that too much sleep is a big problem- most especially when opportunity is all around you. A man who sleeps during the harvest will become poor. You cannot fold up your arms and close your eyes, snoring, when others are busy doing something profitable. If you are that kind of person, opportunities will pass you by, and if you're not careful, the little that you have will also be taken from you.

DON'T SLEEP YOUR LIFE OFF

Sleeping does not necessary mean lying down on the bed closing your eyes. Some people can have an 'I don't care.' attitude which can lead to poverty. Every single day of their life, they cannot be bothered. When they see an open door to their awaiting privilege, instead of running to it, they are too cool and easy until the opportunity finally slips through their hand. Before they awake into reality, regret is their order of the day.

No matter how powerful you may be if you employ a sleeping man as your security or gatekeeper, you will soon be captured by your enemy. If you are the sleeping person, your chance of making money will be difficult. Sleeping habits can destroy a lot of relationships and cause confusion among brethren. Many are not able to achieve their desirable dream because of too much sleeping.

According to studies, if you are given 100 years to live on this earth, and you sleep the normal traditional 8 hours per day, you have already slept for 25 years, which means you only have 75 years left to acquire your success.

STEP OUT OF SLEEPING HABITS

I remember, some time ago, one of the members of my ministry, named Steve, worked in a security company in central London. His job was very hectic because he worked as a night security officer. He was in charge of guarding one of the busy CCTV companies all night long, including weekends and sometimes on public holidays.

Meanwhile, in one of my seminars, I preached that "If you are not happy with your current situation, be tough, go ahead, and change it! The power is in your hand." I mentioned that if you want to do the impossible, you need to do the impossibility; this statement challenged him. Although Steve only got eight hours sleep which is the average recommended by the doctor, to my surprise Steve decided to cut his sleeping hours from eight to four. The remaining four hours he used to further his education by registering in a school for a special course. As of today, he has already acquired the necessary qualification. Steve is making more money and living a better life.

4. HASTY PERSON

The plans of the diligent lead surely to plenty, but those of everyone who is hasty, surely to poverty. **Prov.21:5**

As the saying goes, slow and steady wins the race. Sad enough, some people - especially the young stars of today, want to live in the fast lane without knowing that the faster you run, the faster you will become tired. William Wills (Gambling centre) opened up a place for such people who wake up early in the morning and line up to gamble in the hope that they can get rich quickly. The irony of life is that wealth only comes to those who are steady. As you know, slow and steady wins the race. If you are in a hurry to get money, it's possible to make it quickly, but the way it comes is the same way in which it will disappear.

Anybody who is in a hurry to make money will do anything to get it. They can use any means to achieve their aims. I heard a story of a man who conspired with his wife to sell their baby for the sake of making money. While they were about to collect the money in exchange for their baby, the police came and arrested them both. Instead of making money, they were put behind bars. The little baby grew up and became rich but was sadly unable to look after the parents due to the evil they had planned for him.

IF YOU RUSH IN, YOU MAY RUSH OUT

The prisons are full of young adults, some of them as young as 15 years of age, serving long jail sentences for drug trafficking. What a wasted life!

Some will even go as far as engaging in black magic or African voodoo in order to get money. Nowadays, in Europe, the numbers of people playing the Lotto are numerous. No wonder the levels of poverty are increasing every day. There is also a seminar around the city promising people that they can make money quickly. A number of fraudulent young people are surfing the internet from the middle of night until early morning doing yahoo.com (sending messages which offer millions to any victim who wishes to get rich out of their fake promises). They have devoted their life to such unscrupulous schemes which make it impossible to make money honestly. If you ever hurry to make money, you will be poor. If you are going to undertake a get -rich -quick program, you are just going to poverty lane room 131. Do not get money quickly to avoid poverty.

5. A MOCKER OR DESPISER OF PEOPLE

Blessed is the man who walks not in the counsel of the ungodly, nor stands in the path of sinners, nor sits in the seat of the scornful. **Psalm. 1:1**

Life demands an appreciation, what you cannot do others can. Tiger Woods may not be able to play football like David Beckham or sing like Lionel Richie but when it comes to golf history, he is champion amongst golfers. Life is full of variety. Where some are successful, others will be failures. Some may not be able to be the king of the night, but their little star in the sky makes a great difference in the darkness.

No matter what may be your incapability, when you see those who are capable they deserve to be celebrated and whatever you celebrate, you are able to attain. From the history of the world, people who despise others end up in the bottomless pit with their ends in great ruin. No matter how hard they try, things never work out. Mockers will belittle every opportunity around them. Whenever they see someone who is rich, they gossip about their riches. Mockers rise up early to travel miles in order to spoil their fellow human beings. If they ever smile, they really are crying and their yes stands for no. A riches begat riches as the proverb goes. Most people who are mockers end up being always poor and it will be impossible for people around them to help as their deeds are noticed.

Whatever you despise you not derive; when you wish your brother good luck, others will wish you the same in life. If you see a brother or a sister whom God has done something new for and you are not happy, welcome to poverty lane. If you see a newly wedded couple, congratulate them and do not be jealous. Don't despise people; be careful of how you react to other people's success. In other words do not sit in a position of mockery. Don't despise people who succeed or else you will become poor in life.

6. IGNORANT

My people are destroyed for lack of knowledge. Because you have rejected knowledge, I also will reject you from being priest for me;

because you have forgotten the law of your God, I also will forget your children **Hosea 4:6**

To be ignorant means to lack knowledge. Money making is a matter of common sense but unfortunately sense is not common. If you are able to use your brain, you will be rich, but when you are not well informed, you only go round in circles. Where others are successful you will be lacking. Many people in life suffer in silence- not because they have no one to assist them to get to the top or because they are not well-connected. Rather, people become poor only for the fact that while they were so close to many opportunities in life, they were not be able to do the right thing at the right time. The ignorant are full of foolishness, and they reason with their left brain.

OPPORTUNITIES ARE EVERYWHERE

Life is full of many opportunities. The more you recognize what is by your side, the better you discover many others in your surroundings. Always remember: successful information is everywhere, only the wise will use their common sense to position themselves for great privilege. No man is born with poverty. You may be borne to poor people or raised by poor relatives but these are not guarantees that you will be poor for the rest of your life. For your information, the majority of the millionaires you see today were not born rich; they became rich as the result of fighting a battle against ignorance. They educated themselves about moving from the bottom to the top. Life may not be fair, but situations can be changed. It all depends on how you handle your situation. No man can take you to where you want to be unless you move yourself forward through the information you gathered. Then, you are able to make use through your entire life.

SEE THE INVISIBLE TO DO THE IMPOSSIBLE

Many people are very comfortable with their unwanted circumstances, while others refuse to accept defeat over victory and move the vehicle of rejection to the place of acceptance. They'ill start doing what will profit the future rather than clinging to the past where they've experienced failure.

Many things usually lead to ignorance. The fear of failure, the ability not to be able to trust people after they have been betrayed or after someone has moved their milestone to other locations, and many other reasons. This problem is better known, to those who have suffered these experiences, as ignorance. Ignorance will debar you from progress; it will stop you from moving to the place of assignment and connect you to the wrong side of life. Ignorance will forbid you to see the invisible and where you cannot see the invisible you cannot do the impossible.

Ignorance is an act of foolishness; many will die of ignorance before they realize what they have missed out in life. What you do not know is what made others to be rich. Foolishness will lead to poverty.

7. FOOLISHNESS

Poverty resides in the bosom of a fool. Where the wise survive, the foolish will perish. Foolishness is the opposite of wisdom. The bridge between the rich and the poor is wisdom and where wisdom is applied, money will surface. Likewise, where foolishness abides, poverty is inevitable. To be a fool means a person who acts in stupidity or lacks good sense of judgment. Give them riches and they will turn these to poverty. Give them a city and they will disastrously reduce it to a hamlet in due season without an apology. Foolishness has nothing to do with age, race, gender or educational background whatsoever. It operates in every category of life, leadership, family, pastor, people or materials. The way of fool is always right in their own eyes; the person who is foolish will not seek advice from others, even if you advise them, they will still end up doing it in their own way. Wise men fear and depart from evil but a fool rages and is self-confident. They will promise you they know what they are doing until everything is messed up and great destruction is their end.

DEPART FROM FOOLISHNESS

If you want to be successful in life never go in the way of a fool as it will hinder your progress in life. The more foolish you are, the more likely is your poverty. The reason why you are suffering financially now is a result of the mistake that happened due to foolishness. The only way out of foolishness is to be aware of your decisions and evaluate your sense of judgment at all times. Pay attention to people around you- most especially those who are already ahead of you. In the mist of many counselors, there is safety. Never depend on your own opinion and don't think you are always right. The wise will build on the rock soil while the foolish build on the sand soil. The wise know that the way to make money is by giving generously, but the foolish withhold their hand which leads to poverty. To learn the hard way means to follow the foolish part of life which will lead to poverty. The foolish see trouble in every obstacle but the wise see opportunity in every trouble, and the trouble you solve will determine the money you have. ***When you have no problems to solve you have no money to spend.***

THE EVIL WORKS OF FOOLISHNESS

There was a lorry driver, who lived in a certain land. He was married with children and loved by people. One day, as he was driving along with his friend, they engaged in conversation about many issues of life and whilst they were driving, the lorry driver told his friend that if petrol is poured on his body he will never get burned.

When the friend realized the conversation was getting out of order, he decided to change the topic but instead the lorry driver got angry and said that his friend did not believe him. After driving a little further he stopped the lorry and got out, he pulled out the petrol container full of unleaded petrol and started pouring it all over his own body. Jokingly, he also took out a fire light from the drawer and handed it to his friend to spark the fire. The friend begged him and told his driver friend the danger behind the evil thought. The lorry driver ignored all the warnings and sparked the naked light which turned him into a fireball. The driver was burned to ashes right there by the road side whilst his friend watched from afar. This incident happened all because of foolishness. If you do not get rid of foolishness, it will take your life from you without any doubt. .

8. PRIDE OR ARROGANCE

Pride *goes* before destruction and a haughty spirit before a fall. Prov.16:18

As the saying goes pride comes before falling. If you have pride in you, it is possible that you may find yourself way up and achieving what you dream in life but the danger is that, no matter how you find your way up, pride will bring you straight down and great will be the destruction. Money will place pride on man as long as you have more than enough.

The problem of humanity even now can be summarized into three categories: Firstly, *THE LUST OF THE FLESH*, secondly, *THE LUST OF THE EYES* and thirdly *THE PRIDE* OF LIFE. Every problem you may encounter in life will fall into any of these three categories. Pride will separate you from all your close friends who can help you to climb the ladder of success. Pride will make you think you know better than everybody around you and the more you think you know better the more you lose information which can generate you money or any progress in life. Humility is the opposite of pride. Wherever there is pride, shame also will follow. People will help the humble to climb up by rendering useful advice that will benefit their life, but much information will be withheld from anyone with pride. Do you want to acquire money? Stay humble and be connected to your destiny.

THE POWER OF SIGHT
Pride will retain you in the lowest pit of life (Pro.29:23)
The purpose of sight is the ability to see clearly. The more you see the better you can perform. What you see is what you acquire. You can become anything in life, if only you can see and the only way to see clearly is to humble yourself before people around you. Stay calm; as we all know slow and steady win the race.

God can only help those who are humble. He reveals witty ideas which will get them to the wealthy place.

There will always be a place where you will be crowned with success. A place where all your labor will be rewarded and people will gather to celebrate your new life. A place where money is never a scarcity, where all your visions become reality and you will be dining with all the nobles in the land. The secret to that place is hiding inside humility and not in pride or arrogance. *The story of most millionaires you see around you started from humility and the more they stay humble the better they retain their wealth.* Whoever you see at the top, it is not arrogance or pride that got them there. The secret is hiding in humility. Although when you have money, pride is included in the package, it is your duty to get the pride out of your life. If not, poverty will be attached with arrogance and pride. After all, what is it that you have that others have not got?

9. PROCRASTINATION.
They sow the wind, and reap the whirlwind. The stalk has no bud; wind it shall never produce meal. If it should produce, Aliens would swallow it up **Hosea.8:7**
Procrastination will lead to poverty, in the sense that if what needs to be achieved presently is put off till another day without any solid reason, the result will be a lack and a lack is poverty. Procrastination is a virus, the ability to postpone things. You say to yourself - I will do it tomorrow; forgetting that tomorrow may never come. For the majority of people in our society today that are not successful, it's not because they do not have knowledge or great ability to make it in life. . The problem is conceived in the womb of procrastination.

TIME IS MONEY

Money is a currency which flows all across. The quicker you see it, the better you make use of what you see, but the moment you feel you are taking your time is the moment when somebody snatches the opportunity from you. This has left many people stranded and most of the time such people become poor.

The time you decide what to do will determine how successful you will become. As you know, time is money and time waits for no one. To prove it, answer this question: You are not in the same age as you were yesterday, are you? You may not be able to correct your past, but you can get hold of today for the benefit of tomorrow. Whatever needs to be done has to be done right now and the more you make use of now, the more gainfully you acquire opportunities in life.

RICH PEOPLE ARE RISK TAKERS

The Earth is full of people who are looking for the same privilege as you. You may not see the full light yet, but noticing a little never wastes time. Go for it! You will soon discover that a little drop of water becomes a mighty ocean. Never get confused. Life is about risks and the bigger your risk, the more you make money. Rich people are risk takers and not procrastinators. The today you see is better than the tomorrow you are banking on. The ability to start small is a sign of seriousness. The one step you take is better than thousand steps you are planning to take in the future. Don't get me wrong, your future is very important- it will be the finishing point of your life - but the today you see is better than tomorrow you have not entered. If you want to be rich, do something right now that will guarantee you a better tomorrow.

ALWAYS GET YOUR PRIORITY RIGHT

Many people are poor because they neglect today for their tomorrow, hoping and planning for another day when they could make use of the day they have at hand. Some people have the habit of postponing the most important things in their life until another day. Why wait for tomorrow when you can get it done today?

There was a particular story of man who went to a family friend to ask for a favor which was very important to him. Upon his arrival, the family friend ordered the man to eat first before making his request known. The man sat down and ate first.

Meanwhile another visitor came to ask for a favor from the friend and was also asked to settle down and eat before he makes his request known. The visitor refused and got straight to the point without procrastination. The first visitor, who was eating, later finished the meal and decided to make his intention known. Sadly, the family friend told the man it was too late as the other visitor came for the same purpose and was granted his request first. Regrettably, the man left minus the favor.

When you procrastinate in life you will miss your opportunity.

I have never seen anyone who procrastinates and is still successful. The plan in your heart is not what you should defer for another time. Now is the time. Successful people never delay chances. The chances you delay will be the opportunity you will never possess.

Procrastination will lead to poverty.

HOW TO ACQUIRE MONEY SUMMARY

- *A SUCCESSFUL PERSON HAS LITTLE TO TELL ABOUT THE TRUE STORY OF SUCCESS, BUT YOU CAN LEARN A GREAT DEAL FROM THE LESSONS OF A FAILURE.*
- *THE OPPOSITE OF MONEY IS LACK WHICH CAN ALSO BE CALLED POVERTY OR STATE OF BEING POOR.*
- *POVERTY COMES AS A RESULT OF LITTLE MISTAKES. POVERTY IS NOT A DESIRE; RATHER IT'S AN ACT OF FOOLISHNESS.*
- *THE BRIDGE BETWEEN THE POOR IN OUR SOCIETY AND THE RICH PEOPLE IS WISDOM PRINCIPLES.*
- *POVERTY IS VERY BAD AND IF CARE IS NOT TAKEN, A BELIEVER CAN DENY HIS ALMIGHTY GOD.*
- *PROVERTY WILL DENY YOU OF LIFE'S BENEFITS AND SEPARATE YOU FROM FRIENDS AND RELATIVES.*
- *TO BE POOR MEANS YOU HAVE FAILED IN LIFE AND THERE IS NO EXCUSE FOR FAILURE. PROVERTY IS A MATTER OF THE MIND.*
- ***YOUR PRIORITY WILL DETERMINE YOUR LIVING MENTALITY.***
- *POVERTY IS LIKE A VIRUS. IF NOT PROPERLY TREATED, IT COULD AFFECT A WHOLE GENERATION, EVEN ONTO THE NEXT GENERATION.*
- *POVERTY IS A CAUSE AND THE ONLY WAY OUT IS TO BREAK OUT OF IT.*
- *REMEMBER GOD PROFITS NOTHING FROM A FAILURE, BUT HE DELIGHTS IN THE PROSPERITY OF HIS PEOPLE.*

BASIC THINGS THAT LEAD TO POVERTY

1. LOVER OF PLEASURE - *PRO. 21:17*
2. LAZINESS - *PRO. 20:4*
3. TOO MUCH SLEEP- *PRO.20:13*
4. HASTY PERSON- *PRO.21:5*
5. MOCKER OR DISPISER OF PEOPLE. -*PSALM 1:1*
6. IGNORANCE -*HOSEA 4:6*
7. FOOLISHNESS -
8. PRIDE OR ARROGANCE -*PRO.16:18*
9. *PROCRASTINATION.-HOSEA 8:7*

CHAPTER TWO
UNDERSTANDING MONEY

(GEN 31: 1-18)
If you want to know what God thinks of money, just look at the people he gave it to. Dorothy Parker (1893 - 1967)

WHAT IS MONEY? Money is a legal tender, currency that is used to settle debts or payment for goods and services. However each country has its own legal tender. You cannot spend pounds sterling in America; it has to be converted into dollars in order for the money to be spent. Money is a legal tender, that's why if you take a look at the note, for example it says I promise to pay the bearer on demand the sum of £20 so I can only settle the debt of £20 with the note but if the debt amounts to £40, I then need another £20 note to settle this debt. Money is a legal tender used to settle debt in exchange for goods and services.

I remember when I was in Germany, my sister promised to send me 300,000 lire and I was happy, only to realize that 300,000 lire was just £100 at the time of exchange. Before I received the money, I thought my sister was rather rich, it was only later I realized the true value of that currency.

You can't go into petrol station and tell them you want to buy petrol with your love, you would be chased out. If you can seduce the salesman, you cannot seduce the manager; if you seduce the manager, you cannot seduce the owner. The only way you can have a good security is by paying for what you need.

THE TRUTH ABOUT MONEY
The truth you know about money will determine how good you will possess money. **John 8: 32** say *"you will know the truth and the truth will make you free."*

My question is what if you don't know the truth; the answer is you will be enslaved. Many of us do not know the truth about where we stand in our finances. You say 'but 'no' I am free, I'm not enslaved'. You are enslaved by the time you get to a shop, you are demanding to buy something and your money is not up to its standards. Just like when I was in Germany; I went to make a phone call. It was very expensive back then, not like today, where cheap communication is easily available. I went out on a cold winter day to make a phone call to my wife who was living back in Nigeria. As I was communicating with her, she began to tell me a good story which I had missed. I put more money into the pay phone box while my wife was still narrating more interesting stories. I was left with just enough money to use for my transportation. Because I was enjoying listening to her, I put the whole of my transportation money into the phone box which swallowed it. I needed to travel about 10 km to get home, so I had to walk. Although I enjoyed listening to my wife's story, the fact is the phone company made quite a lot of money from me. They exchanged their service for the sake of allowing me to communicate to my wife. In other words, the truth you know about money will determine how about good you will possess it.

MONEY IS EVERYWHERE

Some of us don't know anything about money the attitude we have towards money is so bad that money is running away from us. You must know the truth about money; you must know how to identify money. Let me tell you the truth; money is everywhere! Money is in the place where you are right now, but because you don't know the truth, you walk past it, you jump past it and you never have it. For you to see money you must open your inner eye (vision) and also open up and broaden your understanding. You have to see beyond where you are; you have to see great opportunities. Do you ever ask yourself this question; why do some people have a bank account and their account never goes in the red? The bank balance sheet is always in the black. Every day they issue fat cheques, ride the most expensive latest car in town, live in the best house and they are financially free. It's because they know the truth about how to acquire money. Instead of being financially illiterate, they are financial educated. The role of money is very important in society and you have to understand how to make more money so that you can stay on top.

WHAT MAKES THE DIFFERENCE

The difference between the rich and poor is wisdom. What you are doing is the same as what they are doing. The job you are doing is same as what they are doing. People are broke and shattered due to lack of understanding. Now I say money does not have mouth, but she speaks every language of the world and people understand the language because everybody needs money. *Eccl. 10:19* says *"A feast is made for laughter, and wine makes merry; but money answers everything"*.

If you love to do something very important and it does not work, it means you have no money. Money in your hand will make you rule the world. Go to any political organization in any giving state or county and show them the millions you have with solid evidence, you will be surprised how this can make you one of the leaders of their land. Everybody needs money and money is power. It's the only thing that doesn't have a mouth yet speaks every language of the world. If you go to China, Italy or any part of the world and you bring out money, it will definitely be understood as to what you need. They may not know who you are right now but when your money comes you will need no introduction; just be diligent in what you are doing and watch how your head will be lifted up. It's just a matter of time.

NOT HARD WORKING BUT SMART WORKING

Money can be viewed in two perspectives, either you see her as your slave or the master of your life. For example, how many times do you refuse some projects because you don't have the money? Many people are enslaved to money, they work so hard to get it, but can I tell you, stop working hard for money. If working harder is what brings money, then grave diggers would be the richest people in the whole world, but the truth is most of them are shattered and broke. If the greatest millionaire should exist in life, then it should be the security officer or a toilet cleaner because they put the most effort into their work. Some of them work round the clock but at the end of the day they have little or nothing to show for their hard working. Whereas on the other side, only a small boy with a mobile phone and laptop, white shirt in black suit with a tie, clean and sparkling, working smartly and putting wisdom together and before you know money keeps coming like a flowing river. For you to acquire money is not by working hard but working smartly. Money is a servant. I call money an errand boy and to those who understand the rule of servant hood, the character you display at present of your servant will determine how effective it will behave toward you.

Money is ready to bow down to you, coming in groups of thousands and millions if you can understand the secret, that is, the ability to use money or send money in the right direction but if you position yourself as a slave, money will be otherwise taking control of people's lives. Dictate when to wake up and when to sleep, where to go, what not to do. Money has become the chief commanding officer to most people in society; beautiful marriages are being shattered every single day all because of money issues. You either control money or money controls you. The answer is not what you say out of your mouth but the action surrounding the life you live.

The main reason why I write this book is to show you the secret which I called the missing link so as to enable you to acquire your desired money.

MONEY LOVES TO STAY IN THE RIGHT PLACE

Money can only stay in an environment which is compatible or sustainable and the more you know, the better the money keeps coming in. Money does not like to stay in a rough place where there is no security. Whenever you put money in your house, you will need to constantly check that the doors are secure, no matter the amount of the money you will always double check your actions. However, when you put money into a bank, the bank is using your money by giving out loans to people who use it for business purposes. The bank will collect interest, making more money out of the finance you kept in their care. The hardest work they have to do is to update the account, keep the paper work in order and they are the more successful. Money is only compatible to stay in safe environment and the more you keep it in the right place the greater the reward. Do you know that money beckons to money. When £1000 knows you are here, it calls out for another £1000, it depends on your understanding toward the use of money. Do you know the bible says **the rich will become richer and the poor poorer**. Why? Because the more money you have in your pocket, the better the chances of making an investment, that's what I mean by compatibility. This will not work, though, if you acquire £1000 and the first thought that comes to your mind is to spend the money, this is the major problem for people in our society and the outcome is poverty.

MONEY IS MADE TO BE INVESTED

Do you remember what I said about the mind-set of the poor people Who say "money is meant to be spent"? No, money is not meant to be spent but money is meant to be saved, although there are times you need to spend money. However, it is important to invest your money and get an understanding on how money can work for you. If you don't understand money, you are wasting your time, no matter the prayer; you are only wasting your energy. I remember those days when I did not have understanding of money. I was broke and shattered, but now I understand the principle of money and I want you to be informed so as not to make the same mistakes. The secret of the rich people is the habit they possess towards money and they devote their life on these habits every time. You just have to understand money.

MATT. 25:16-17 Jesus told us about the story in the bible of a man who was going on a journey. He gave some people money, one man got five, another two and the last person got one but the one that had five understood what money was all about. He quickly went and traded with his five. What happened is that he had five and came back with ten. Money is currency which needs to flow around and come back with interest. The bible says **the righteous shall flourish like a palm right tree**; you have to see yourself moving far beyond your early morning or any ordinary menial job.

JUST TAKE IT EASY

Life is more than a struggle or fight for survival. The fact is money is not only about the legal paper in the circulation but money is the ability to render service as a medium of exchange. *The idea in your mind is bigger than any money available at hand.* You just have to get your priorities right. It is shameful enough that some people purposely beg their boss to give them overtime work to cover bills, which is very hazardous to human health instead of taking rest, travel or going on a holiday.

There was a story of a young man in Germany; whose name is Ade. He came to Germany and was working in a farm owned by a German farmer. Ade worked so hard even during the winter when everywhere was freezing. The young African man still carried on working in the cold. One day the boss asked why he carried on with this tedious task and to cut the long story short, Ade had to lie to his boss just because he needed that job badly. The boss was surprised and later asked this young African boy to visit a doctor for medical check-up as the guy was sweating heavily in the cold weather.

The guy booked an appointment with the doctor. The doctor told him that his brain had frozen and that he had got 3 days to live. Subsequent to all his hard working and struggling, he died on the third day. After the death of this young man DM12,000 (German money) approximately

£6,000 was found in his room. The irony of this story is that the mother and the wife of the man fought over the money for a whole decade.

The bible says what profits a man to gain the whole world and lose his own soul. Please just take things easy in life, there may not be enough money now but watch out money is coming.

THE POWER OF VISION

The money I am talking about here is the money that would promote you, the money that will take you to another level. I see that money coming into your hands. Although money is physical, you need the spiritual eyes and knowledge before you can acquire money. When I say spiritual eyes, I am talking in terms of your vision, creativity, ideas or imagination. If you do not have vision, you cannot see money. Only visionaries see money. I remember a story of two friends who travelled to India and while they were in Bombay, one of them saw people with no shoes on their feet, and felt pity, but the other one saw an opportunity. He determined to manufacture shoes and send them to India? So both men went to India, one saw people with no shoes and the other saw a vision of how to put shoes on the peoples' feet. Today this man is one of the billionaires in our generation. Money can only come when you are able to a solve problem, when others see certain things as an obstacle, other people take on the role of problem solver and once you have learned how to a find solution to the problem, that is the time you will make more money.

Some people will say they are Christians, they prefer to die and go to Heaven. To be honest and truthful some will get to heaven with the baggage of poverty, even when they die by the time they get there, God may send them back, because heaven street is full of gold and because they have never been used to such a glittery environment, then heaven will becomes scary to such people.

MONEY IS IN EVERY PROBLEM YOU SOLVE

Hairdresser makes money for fixing untidy hair, barbers make money for fixing rough hair, doctors make money by solving health problems, mechanics solve car problems, undertakers tackle the problem of the dead, shoe companies make money because people need shoes, and the list of traders solving everyday problems goes on forever. *The problem you solve will determine the money you acquire*. This is the very reason why you should not run away from any difficult task, the more problems you solve in life, the more money you will possess.

What things do you see or hear, what thoughts do you have or words come out of your mouth? Remember you are not on the Earth by accident; you are here to address certain issues. The earlier you discover your assignment the more money you will acquire. You just have to know who you are. Any time you think you don't have any money it means you lack problems to solve, if you need money, look for problems to solve. After all, a footballer needs to look for a team and will go to the football field kicking a ball before any money arrives.

DISCOVER YOURSELF

Whatsoever that is your pain will become your passion, your passion will help you to climb the ladder to the top. Any time you discover pain in your heart, something is about to take place. Pain itself is not a problem it's only a pointer to the direction of what the matter is. Pain will help you to pay a special attention to what has gone wrong and to remind you to be careful with the way you handle things.

Unfortunately, today everybody is running away from pain. *You need to go through the pain barrier before you can have the message.*

Gold is precious and valuable due to the fire it has gone through. Whatever pain is in your heart, it will give you the opportunity to find a solution. Do you know that even the way you are laughing now, is a solution to somebody? Take a look at comedians; they tell a joke, it makes you laugh and you paid to see their show. All you need to give to David Beckham is just football, he has legs the same as yours, and he doesn't have 3 heads. Obama is a man like you, and the bible says Elijah is a man just like us, he doesn't have 7 heads.

Money is not only physical but you need to see it in the vision; you need to have a dream. Please don't wake up in the morning without any vision. Some spend their time without any vision, some have wasted the best time of their life doing nothing or unprofitable things when they have the capability, no wonder now they work like a cow with a disease.

WHAT DO YOU SEE?

Some people saw a drunkard and some were thinking what they can do to get the alcohol off their hands. You need to see a solution in every surface problem and fix it not by running away or getting scared. Every man is created by God to solve another man's problem. I don't know how you see yourself, but that's how you can make money. You've got to understand that money does not come easily. Money comes as a result of your vision and dreams with your passions. Don't always complain about things but get ready to find solutions. ***Money cannot produce wisdom but wisdom will produce money.*** Some people see nothing but trouble. They complain, grumble, and are bitter all the days of their life.

No wonder money cannot come to such people; you have to understand the wave of money. A bad attitude toward money will result in lack of money. If you have a good attitude toward money, believe me money will flow all around you and my prayer is that God will increase your wisdom, ability, understanding in all areas of life. A respectful attitude matters in life. I remember some time ago, someone asked why most black churches don't have white members, is it because they are too lively. What's lively? If playing music drives away white people then why are we playing music, why don't you change the music or start a new service where there is no music and preach only the gospel. Do you know the bible says wisdom is the principle thing. Why do homes break?? It is because of lack of wisdom. You lose money easily because you lack wisdom but when you have wisdom, this will bring money. I will dwell on wisdom when we get to the section on how to acquire money itself. It's a principle key which I will talk more about later.

GET THE POWER TO MAKE MONEY

Money is a product of mankind but the power to make it belongs to the Almighty God. ***Deut.8:18*** says ***"And you shall remember the LORD your God, for it is He who gives you power to get wealth that He may establish His covenant which He swore to your fathers, as it is this day"***.

The power of God the bible is talking about here is not just your ability or your strength, but about the power of your thinking. Great riches lie in the power of your mind. Many of you are aware of SKY TV or a satellite provider. Do you remember that it was impossible before to rewind, forward and pause while watching your favorite programme on sky digital TV channel? Unfortunately what most people do is to change from one station to the other, flipping from soap opera to films or whatsoever, but somebody calculated the possibility of how to record programmes with this new technology. Do you realize that today all these questions had been answered by somebody who is now making huge amounts of money from this latest discovery What was impossible yesterday is now possible through the power of the mind.

New technologies are being discovered every day, unbelievable idea through the minds of people either young or old, this power is available to all from God, all you need is get closer to God and you can discover yours. God works through our brain by dropping useful information which will allow us to acquire money. We should not let those visions and dreams die, as they can create great wealth. Those ideas you think are just ordinary, they are not. They are special; they are the power to success.

USE YOUR BRAIN

Psychologically, it has being recorded that more than 1,500 ideas come to our brain every day, however, they vanish because they are not recorded. How many good songs are out there that we have not yet heard. What happened is that you thought about the idea but you let it go. You convince yourself you are not a good singer. Do you know, majority of the musicians are not good singers. Neither are they composers, do you know that R. Kelly (American Artiste) does not write some of his songs, and that someone is paid to write material for him. What has happened to the songs that you have created, what about the great stories that could make good movies. Useful information can benefit our planet and procrastination will rob you of present and future opportunities. Can I tell you the truth that the greatest richest men on earth are in the graveyard lying down buried with their vision; you will not die with your dreams.

ACCESS THE HEAVENLY INFORMATION

Always remember, the power to make wealth or achieve things is still in the hands of God. Sometimes God wants you to sleep or take a rest so that he can show you more revelations that will profit your future but instead we are sometimes too busy doing unprofitable things in life. Information can come into your spirit at any time which will develop into marvelous ideas. The book of **Joel 2:28** says ***on the last days, I will pour out my spirit upon all flesh***.

The spirit of the Lord gives you access to heavenly information and it depends on how you handle the situation before you can have great opportunities. It also depends on using your intuition. Do you know those things in your heart are from God? The desire of God is for all men to be successful and live a better life. He has loaded all of us with daily benefits and assigned individuals with unique gifts. God is the road map to all our success, no matter who you are as long as you follow His principal success and the instruction which is already laid down in the manual (Holy-Bible) you will definitely make it.

ADJUST YOUR MINDSET

Wrong mind-set will lead to lack of money but a right mind-set will produce an abundance of money as it depends on how you think about money. What are your dreams? People say they are not interested in money because their mind-set is wrong, your mind-set has to be right before you can acquire money for your choices. Actually most people inherit their mind-set from their parents When a mother tells her children that every single man is bad, it is because the children's father maybe abused her. Now just because of one man, her thinking is that all men are bad. This statement will block her daughter from marrying the right person and many good men will walk pass her without paying any attention again. Excuse me! Bad mentality will lead to scarcity, if your mind is not right, your life will not be okay because success is a matter of mind your attitude toward life is all about your mind, failure or progress is in your mind. You can read all the books from great authors and attend seminars and lectures from all the great leaders. However, if your mind is not right you only feel good for a short time and after a while you will return to a wrong, confusing life. When it comes to money matters, you need the right mind, as I previously said, money is everywhere and money is in everything.

THE SECRET OF MONEY

The secret of acquiring money is the ability to see it and if your mind is wrong even when you see money you don't know what it is. The Bible says *renewing your mind daily so that you can do what is acceptable ... Rom.12:2*

Most people think only those who are fortunate can make money or some naturally gifted people have the power to make money. Some believe you have to work hard doing 9:00am - 5:00pm before you can make it, No; there are many ways to make money, and I will show you how.

Please have this in your mind; before you can make money, you need to understand the principles surrounding money.

Prov.11:24 - 25 "one man gives freely, yet gains even more; another withholds unduly, but come to poverty. A generous man will prosper; he who refreshes others will himself be refreshed.

YOU HAVE TO GIVE TO RECIEVE

Do you know that some people when you are calling out to sow a seed in the church or Christian gathering, they see it like they have come again and they say all they need is our money. That's why they are still poor. Not only that, some people come and say can you lend me £20 and they will return it later. Although you have the money, you say I don't have it, you have forgotten that the more you give, the more you get. Don't be like a brother, who had a few coins in his hands and they wanted to give him £50 and he says I can't let go, I've got too much money and how much are the coins, just £13. You have to know the principle of giving, to stay out of poverty Never be ignorant you have to know the secret. The principle is that you have to give to receive. If you know this your fortune will change. What does it cost you? To find the answer to your question, it's in your understanding which can be derived from others' experiences. Why not go and study carefully? Read books and when you get this secret you will be free from a poverty mentality but above all, keep your mind open to change and new experiences.

HOW TO ACQUIRE MONEY SUMMARY

- MONEY CAN ONLY STAY IN AN ENVIRONMENT COMPATABLE TO RETAIN HER AND THE MORE YOU KNOW THE BETTER MONEY KEEPS COMING. **MATT.25:16-17**
- ALTHOUGH MONEY IS PHYSICAL, YOU NEED THE SPIRITUAL EYE (VISION) AND KNOWLEDGE BEFORE YOU CAN ACQUIRE HER. **GEN. 31:10**
- MONEY MAY NOT PRODUCE WISDOM BUT GREAT WISDOM WILL PRODUCE MONEY AND RETAIN HER. **PRO.4:8-9**
- MONEY IS A PRODUCT OF MANKIND BUT THE POWER TO MAKE IT BELONGS TO THE ALMIGHTY GOD. **DEUT. 8:18**
- WRONG MINDSET WILL LEAD TO LACK OF MONEY BUT RIGHT MIND WILL PRODUCE AN ABUNDANCE OF MONEY. **ROMANS 12:1-2**
- BEFORE YOU CAN MAKE MONEY YOU NEED TO UNDERSTAND THE PRINCIPLES SURROUNDING MONEY. **PROVERBS. 11:24-25**

CHAPTER THREE
THE LIES OF MONEY

It has been said that the love of money is the root of all evil. The want of money is so quite as truly. Samuel Butler (1835 - 1902)

In the event of lies, every fact seems so real and truthful, it will sound familiar but in the end it's one of those things . The truth about any lie is that, if careful investigation and thorough research is not done, coupled with time taken into consideration, the truth may not be found but when there is evidence, every lie will eventually be exposed. There are many things you've heard about money that are lies, and there are also many truths you should know about money.

KNOWING YOUR RIGHT

How many of you know the Lord has blessed you, the day you were born from your mother's womb according to **Genesis. 1:28** says *"then God blessed them, and God said to them, "Be fruitful and multiply; fill the earth and subdue it; have dominion over the fish of the sea, over the birds of the air, and over every living thing that moves on the earth".*

You are princes and you are princesses. God calls us out of darkness into his marvelous light. The day you gave your life to Jesus, you automatically became one of the members of the kingdom. The bible says apparently, you are no longer a foreigner, but you are a fellow citizen of heaven, so you have the right to command everything including the ability to acquire money in the kingdom. Only servants beg, where the word of king is, there is authority. There was a story about a man in the Bible who had great riches and one of his sons said "Daddy, I am tired of poverty, I am a man, and I also need my own settlement". What happened, his father did not deny him, his father gave him his own portion but along the line, after grabbing the money he went to another country and wasted it. So he came back broke and shattered but praise God we have a father who always cared. A kiss of an enemy becomes an abomination but the kiss of a friend is very sweet.

GET THE JUNK OUT OF YOUR HEAD

For many decades the society has been lying to us. We have not been told the truth about money, even in our educational system. You may have been to many schools, and studied in business or banking, but still you are not informed about the real truth of money. All they teach you is just go and work hard, get many clients, after you finish your degree, then live a life, rent a house and get married. At the end of the day do you still receive the money? Some of you are university graduates and you are still shattered and broke. You have studied at Cambridge, you studied at Oxford, you have studied many subjects and at the end of the day, you are still your normal self. Our heads are filled with junk which we are finding difficult to erase and we are busy transferring junk information to our children. The junk your mum learned is transferred to you, but I have an announcement, the bible says mother or father will no longer eat grapes and leave the mouth of the daughter sour. Whatsoever anything your mother or your father or even the country you come from has planted into your head which does not allow you to make your desirable money, today as a prophet of the Lord, I decree that God will destroy them completely, transform you by the renewing of your mind.

WHATSOVER YOU ASK YOU SHALL RECEIVE

For your understanding, Satan is a liar, the father of all lies. There are so many things he has programmed into the mind of people, most especially believers who love God with all their heart. Through certain teachings from the preachers of the gospel either still living or dead, some of the teachings are so corrupt and contradicting to the foundation our lord Jesus laid for us to follow; I call it the lies from the pit of hell. I want to congratulate you for reading this book of insight. God himself revealed to me as one of the affected person who had suffered from such lies of the devil but now God has set me free. This book you are reading is not just an idea or a copy of some information which I cooked together in order to present to you for the sake of sales. Of course, as a student myself, I have read many great books and studied under some of the generals in the body of Christ. I have attended many promising seminars, followed many principals and philosophies of life and painful still nothing seem to happen. In this particular book every piece of information is a revelation from above and this was due to my early days when I was still a young boy. I remember praying to God about my future and I said "God all I want in life is just a little money to sustain me".

My prayer was answered, for long time the money in my life was as little as I demanded until few years ago when God gave me a vision which was bigger than I could have imagined and reality chose to appear. I went back to God in prayer, which gave birth to the revelations in this book.

From my personal story you will understand why I write this book.

I want to impact you with knowledge your great grandfather has never taught you. Can I give you a warning, please get a fresh way of thinking because the lies may be already registered in your mind. Unless you stay in the right mind it will be difficult to get understanding in this book, a fresh mind will guarantee a great end. The danger in a mind that is not renewed is that the system within you will be contradicting your ability to gain a new experience because to change the theory of 50 years will not happen in just ordinary one hour.

THESE ARE SOME OF THE LIES

The lies of the devil are some of the statements which people utter from their mouth based on the philosophy of man and not according to the word of God. We use these statements out of ignorance and the truth is that our minds master and focus on these confessions that have the power to limit our performance. Remember you are what you say.

1. MONEY IS MEANT TO BE SPENT

Money is not meant to be spent only but to be saved for investment purpose. For example if you are working and earn £200 a week, you spend £230 and you say to yourself, I will get it next week, that's the reason people stay at the edge of poverty. Our parents never taught us how to save money instead how to spend money, they will tell you 25 reasons why you should spend money but not how to save money. If you earn £200 a week, you are only meant to spend the little fraction of that money. Your earnings are supposed to be divided into parts, one portion for God (Tithe) as commanded by God if you are Christian. One for your family something you reserve this in case your mother calls for money, the third 10% for yourself to take to a restaurant or buy a new shoe or whatsoever, if your 10% is not enough, you can save the 10% up till the when you have enough money to buy what you want, then you have another 30% which is supposed to be the greatest of your money, the 30% you invest into your future, buying shares and saving money in the bank.

2. MONEY IS THE ROOT OF EVIL

Some religious people believe that money is the root of all evil, I know you might have heard people mentioning this statement all around you- no wonder some Christians are running away from the issue of money, this is a lie from the devil, that's why some believers are shattered and broke living below the average life expectancy. Please before you crucify me, kindly study your bible carefully and get an understanding so that you can put Satan where he belongs.

According to **1 Tim 6:10** *"for the love of money is the root of all kinds of evil."* Do you notice that money is not the root of evil but the love of money is. Some people put all their heart into money, to them money is a matter of do or die, they are ready to commit atrocities to one another to acquire money, this is what is to love money which is referred to as the root of evil. Money is supposed to love you and commit to your authority as a messenger, helping you to interpret your God given vision.

Also to love money is to surrender to the commandment of money, in doing so, contradicting your faith and instead of worshiping God you start worshiping money, that's when the bible says it's the root of evil. Money itself is not evil, money is good. Jesus himself in his earthly teaching taught us about money. Go to your index (concordance) check righteousness and finances and tell me if they are equal. If Jesus could teach us about money, who are you to say you don't want to know about money, you don't want to know, yet it is taking over your mortgage, families are shattered, things are falling apart, children disrespecting their parents that shall not be your story. May God give you money that will terminate all these insults.

3. MONEY IS HARD TO MAKE

When something is hard it means it is not right, although the truth is that the mentality of this statement today has driven almost the whole World into working so hard with nothing to show for it. This statement will move your focus from positive to negative, and right direction will lead to wrong motives. Money is not hard to make, it's the simplest thing to make. It's all about your mind and according to the bible *"As a man think in his heart so is he.* When you say to yourself, I am not going to make it, no theologian that can change your mind set, but when you say to yourself, it's so simple, you are working according to your belief, because the word has been programmed in your mind that it is simple. When you say is too hard, then it will be hard for you to make money. You have to see from your inner eye (vision) that money making will be easy for you. Wherever you are located; there is someone who does not sweat running his own business venture, he has already invested around £10,000 into his account for his business. How much do you earn, £7.50 an hour, that's why you think it's hard. If your income is not pleasant you just have to change it by doing something more profitable, you have the ability around you, after all you must see the invisible before you can do the impossible that will lead to extraordinary, you only need to be refreshed. Call deep within yourself and say into your spirit 'money is not hard, it's so simple'. Whatever you think is difficult, it will be difficult and whatever you think is simple will be simple, the principle applies to all things.

4. ONLY THE POOR CAN ENTER HEAVEN

It is easier for a poor man to enter into the kingdom of God than a rich man, *Mark 10:23*, I have heard this statement from poor people who go to church to worship God. This set of people love God so much and are very dedicated, yet in their mind they believe that it is the will of God for them to be poor in order to enter God's kingdom. Can I tell you, it's all lies? What the bible is saying is that when you are poor in the spirit then you will be hungry to acquire the knowledge of God. As I am talking to you now, some of you are poor in your spirit, you want to hear what I'm saying because you need a change in your life and some of you are rich in your thinking and say I don't need this rubbish. The Lord is saying to His people it will be easier for a poor in heart who is completely broken, the poor in heart are always ready to know more, study more, seeking to do the will of God because of the hunger in their heart and by so doing the kingdom of heaven is guaranteed.

To better understand, read **Matthew.5:3** contrary to the belief that it is impossible for the rich to enter the kingdom of God. If you are rich and serve God faithfully, keep to the commandments of God you will surely make heaven. Abraham was a rich man, according to the bible. He enters heaven like many other rich people in the scripture. God delights in the wealth of his people. He gives daily benefits, and you can't serve a big God and stay poor. From the foundation of the earth God already blessed His children. *Gen.1:28*.

YOU CAN DO MORE WITH MONEY

Never look at people who are rich and think they are not going to heaven, can I tell you something, poverty will make you to deny God. King Solomon said *"when you are poor, you can deny God".*

As a rich man or woman you have the right to take authority, money is not going to control your life by telling you when to go or come. The truth is when you are rich you are able to do many things for the lord; you will serve the lord with gladness and have money to do the works of the kingdom. I will talk more about this issue in the importance of money.

Go ahead and make as money as you like after all the earth is of the Lord and the fullness thereof.

5. JESUS CHRIST WAS A POOR MAN

Have you ever heard some religious Seth argue that Jesus Christ was a poor man? If Jesus Christ was a poor man how come he had a treasurer?

For your information Judas Iscariot was Jesus Christ's treasurer. How could a poor man have a treasurer? The donkey he said they should go and bring, do you think it was stolen? Sometimes he instructed his disciples to go to a house where they eat the Lord's Supper, do you know how much is it to hire a classic venue for such activities. Donkeys, in those days, can be compared with a limousine car in our generation, they were very expensive. Poor men didn't ride on donkeys and if you check in your bible, people are quoting the scriptures wrongly. I believe in the bible *2 Corinthians 8:9*, he said Jesus Christ became poor so that we might be rich, not that he was a poor man, no, he became poor so that you might be rich in his death, not financially poor, and he died on the cross so that we may receive the riches of the promises of Abraham. Jesus knows that we are stubborn people, we are rebellious people and many people won't come to church unless something happens to them. When the situation is all right people find it difficult to worship God no matter what you preach to them. Some cannot be bothered until their leg is fixed on the roof and bum is fixed on the machine before they think of God. That's why Jesus came to die for us; he becomes so poor in his death by hanging on the cross for the benefit of our redemption and also to acquire all the blessing of Abraham.

He became poor not because he's a poor man but because of the death on the cross. How many of you know it would take only a humble man to die, he that is proud will not die. Have you ever seen a rich man who says come drive my car and let me go by bus but he takes a man who is humble and that's the reason for Jesus to do that and may the Lord bless your mindset.

6. GET RICH QUICKLY

The generation where we live nowadays is become so frustrating due to the belief that everything should be a quick fix especially the younger generation; they want to be rich immediately, get this straight there is nothing called quick money. ***Prov.21:5***

"***The thoughts of the diligent tend only to plenteousness; but of everyone that is hasty only to want.*** the quicker you make money the quicker you lose it, that's why some people are falling victims. Some people claim to be a money doublers, they promise to double your £1000 to £10,000, and they take advantage of your ignorance and the eagerness which pushes you to make a deposit and at the same time you end up broke and shattered. Some of those things may not be through magic but can I tell you the magic of our generation, do you know who Barclays bank belongs to? You don't know him but you deposit money in his bank. The owner of Barclays bank used to trade in human slavery, selling people to the other slave masters who used them for hard labor but when he realized that slavery was going to be abolished, he discovered that there is still a way to enslave this people through the use of the credit cards in your hands and the loans that you borrow. How many of us have a credit card today. Some people's salaries are not £1000 yet they issue them a credit card with a limit of £2000. People are so quick to go and spend it, before you know it they've decided to go on a holiday they have not planned for, and those who have already fallen victim can tell you how many years it takes to pay back. The £2000 you thought is free, if care is not taken, you will end up paying through your noise. Please never be deceived, stop following the misled by participating on any scheme that promises money to be made quickly. The truth about the lies is that you will end up on the poverty lane and life will become frustrating. This is never the will of God for any one and remember slow and steady win the race.

7. ALL THE CHURCH NEEDS IS MY MONEY

This is another scary lie from the pit of hell and the foundation of this rumor is to destroy the relationship between man and God, hence the devil knows that the more the people of God move closer to the church, where the teachings are of knowing their rights, the better and more successful they are in life.

The church does not need your money; it is you that need the money in the church. Can I tell you there are no amounts of money you can give to the church that is up to the wisdom and the protection of God upon your life. You pay insurance company for your car, you pay council tax, you pay service charge, you pay consultation fee to the lawyer and some of you receive free advice in the house of the Lord. Somebody is confusing your theory by saying that what the church needs is your money, do you know some people are so broke, poor and lack in every knowledge to attain a new level of changing. Instead of them coming closer and hearing the final bandit from their creator through motivated inspirational teaching of the pastor, whom God had been anointed to deliver this message into the heart of such people, the devil is putting these lies in their mind because they think the church needs their money so they don't come to church. Listen to me, the first thing you have to clarify is what is a church? A Church is not a building; we (the people) are the church. So if they say what the church needs is your money how much do you have that can compare to what God has done for you in life. The house where we live is not free,, the electricity, gas, telephone, water bills are not free, likewise the church is not exempted, although some require payments. Some churches might have paid for their building, and some may rent a building, but they still have to meet their bills.

Devil is a liar, I say this and I repeat myself. If what the church needs is money, your prayer should be Lord give me the money to give to the church. A time is still coming when you alone on behalf of your family will come to show your gratitude in the church by donating the sum of one million pound and you tell your pastor; please don't announce my name and that shall be your story.

Just like I said before, people who are poor, when it comes to money they don't want you to talk about it, why? Because they are poor, but a rich man is thinking what can he do to appreciate the goodness of God in his life and whatsoever they have given to support the projects of the church. They are not always satisfied, they just want to help in all diverse areas, either to change the equipment or the instruments, support the evangelical teams, the charity arms of the church or even to send a man of God to the holiday of their dreams. A rich man wants to use his money to bless the house of God. May the Lord deliver you from every poverty mentality.

8. I NEED TO WORK HARD FOR MONEY

I remember the story my parent told me while I growing up. They woke me up very early in the morning and advised me with passion *"Please make sure you work hard in your entire life so that you can make enough money"*.

This is the piece of advice every parent will always pass to their children from one generation to another. Even your father and your mother might have told you this same story all over again. This is another lie from the throne of Satan. Can I challenge this theory? If hard working makes money, what happened to the grave diggers? Are they not supposed to be the most successful millionaires on our planet? Are they not working hard, why are toilet cleaners not the richest of all among the office workers? Have you not seen the manager or the boss at the office? All they do is just sit down on the executive leather chair, writing something and throwing paper in the rubbish bin, sometimes they are on the phone communicating and chatting with people on the other end.

Whenever the bell rings or somebody is gaining an entrance to the office the boss only passes a command, by the closing of the day the boss puts some pieces of paper works together and at the end of the month, the hard working cleaner gets paid £6:00per/hour and the boss or manager gets paid around £30 an hour or more. Is this true or false? Hardworking does not make people to be rich; you only need to work smart. Change your mind-set; don't work hard because working hard will keep your brain busy. Work and when money is coming, you will not see it but when you work smart you receive more supernatural information, do you know that smarter people get the right things, their eyes are wide open. Smart people don't just take unnecessary decisions. They are steady and focused, looking for the right avenue that can help them.

When they notice hard work, they delegate people to do it for them and move to another level where money can be acquired more easily. When you work hard all you derive is a little effort and more strength but if you work smart you are very sensitive to situations and can focus on the best result. I will talk about this in the later part for more understanding. God will show you the smartest way to make money.

Let me tell you one of the smartest ways to make money. Footballers don't work hard to make money; they only need a contract and a football field, just to play and score goals, their salary of one week covers some peoples salaries for 20 years . Let me tell you some secrets in life; instead of you concentrating on just what you know and producing less, why not discover your God given gift that will help you to work less in what is not productive. May God grant you the wisdom not to work very hard in your life, but to work smartly.

9. SOME PEOPLE ARE BORN LUCKY TO MAKE MONEY

Most people have given up hope because of this statement. Some people are just born lucky, some people are just very fortunate, it's because he was born in a rich man's house and he can have this and that. Can I tell you the truth, being born in a rich man's house does not determine your riches and there is nobody who is born lucky. Don't let anybody confuse your theory. You all are lucky and I mean blessed. There is no one that is luckier than you, you are not only lucky but you are blessed. Don't let people think that you have to have a certain height, or width before you can make money. That you have to come from a certain country of the world or have a specific stature whatsoever. That you need a peculiar habit before you can be rich. Nobody is born with any habit, character or lucky to acquire money, These are all lies of the devil. Neither is it living in a wealthy nation. All to my imagination, I used to think living in a country such as Great Britain can add to the value of making money with ease, but to my surprise I saw a native English born white man begging for £1 for some chips from me. Do you know those are the things people see and then they think Europeans are better than the Caribbean, African, Chinese or Indian origins, these are all lies! You are born blessed; you have the capacity to be in control of your wealth whichever country you find yourself situated in. It's just a matter of time, and your mind set.

The book of **Ecclesiastes 9:11** says "*I returned and saw under the sun that the race is not to the swift nor the battle to the strong nor bread to the wise nor riches to men of understanding, nor favor to wise no men of skill but chance happen to them all.*

FAVOUR IS NOT FAR

Money making is far more than just being lucky, anybody who follows this principle can be what he wants to be in life and it is not how he started the journey that matters. Some people may be billionaires today and you are still buying your bus pass, but time will tell. I see God promoting you not too long from now. The same house you are living as a tenant, I see you becoming the landlord not because of mortgage but favor will show up, while others are hardworking, favor will just show up for you. Favor is not fair, may God favor you. A favor that transfers the wealth of another man to you. A favor that will place you on a priority list. When others are being ignored, when others are being de-promoted, God will have mercy upon you. So it's not about being born lucky. Nobody is born lucky. We are all born the same. The rich people do not have four eyes, everybody is born just the same.

10. BLAMING THE BIG BROTHER FOR LACK OF MONEY

Recently on our national television, millions of people are all watching a programme where some set of people gather in a house and video cameras record all their activities. Big brother is the name of those who put a camera over your head to watch over you. Big brother can be defined as the government of the land, even your parents for whom you blame your state of poverty on. I tell you, it is very wrong, do not blame your parents for not establishing wealth before you. Mummy made her own mistake and daddy made his own mistake. I tell you God gave birth to you for correction.

Do you know according to history people who win the lottery, still end up being poor. Children who come from rich families may end up in absolute poverty if care is not taken. I tell you, I have seen a man without any history, no family background, from nowhere who became successful, he appeared just like that because he made up in his mind, he did not want to go in the way of his father or sisters as they all are living in complete lack. When you notice your circumstances and life restrictions especially from your environment, you need to drive your life forward and all you need is strong determination. Many rich people are not from a good home or born into a wealth, some of them do not have history relating to money. Those who have good parents and are well brought up can still end up having a divorced home. They find it difficult to cope with their husband and wife, because they think that marriage is an inheritance. Marriage or riches is not an inheritance, it's an investment. You need to invest your time, money and everything. Rather than blaming somebody for your lack or insufficiency all you have to do is to concentrate on how best you can make a difference in any situation you may find yourself. The situation of your country may not be pleasant, yet you can change things around and the more you can solve problems the better you can make money. Big brothers are not your problem they are a solution in my opinion because they will produce the platform for you to shine.

THE SUMMARY OF THE LIES OF MONEY

- FOR MANY DECADES SOCIETY HAS BEEN LYING TO US AND WE HAVE NOT BEEN TOLD THE TRUTH ABOUT MONEY EVEN IN OUR EDUCATIONAL SYSTEM.
- ALL WE HEAR IS THE JUNK IN OUR HEAD WHICH WE ARE FINDING DIFFICULT TO ERASE AND WE ARE BUSY PASSING THIS ON TO OUR CHILDREN.

SOME LIES ABOUT MONEY

- *MONEY IS MADE TO BE SPENT **LUKE 15:14***
- *MONEY IS THE ROOT OF ALL EVIL - **1TIM.6:10***
- *MONEY IS HARD TO MAKE.*
- *IT'S EASIER FOR A POOR MAN TO ENTER INTO THE KINGDOM OF GOD THAN A RICHMAN **MARK 10:23***
- *JESUS CHRIST WAS A POOR O R MAN - **2COR.8:9***
- *I NEED TO GET RICH QUICKLY - **PRO.21:5***
- *ALL THE CHURCH NEEDS IS MY MONEY.*
- *I NEED TO WORK HARD TO MAKE MONEY. WORK . **PRO.23:4***
- *SOME PEOPLE ARE BORN LUCKY TO MAKE MONEY- **ECCL 9:11***
- *BLAMING THE BIG BROTHER FOR LACK OF MONEY*

CHAPTER FOUR
THE TRUTH ABOUT MONEY

If all the rich people in the world divided up their money among themselves there wouldn't be enough to go around. Christina Stead

There are many truths you need to know about money that will give you a better understanding. What is truth? Truth is the evidence of what is reality, that makes you want to know that something is right somewhere. The more truth you know the better you perform and your confidence will increase. Only the truth can create great impact in your life and bring you to a place of reality. Listen to me, lies could take hold of you for a long time, but only one truth will set you free. That's why I say to you, stop listening to people who lie, leave them alone with their lies but one day when the truth is revealed, you will find out that they will be running away when you have found out their lies.

1. MONEY HAS WINGS.

Money has the ability to fly out of your pockets. If you calculate all the salary you have received in one year and all the cheques you've written out, it's possible you could have written over one million pounds. That means you should have become a millionaire by now but some people are still broke. Why? Because the truth is that money or riches can fly away. **Prov.23:5 say that money can fly away.** No matter how you try to keep money in your hand one day you will find that the money is no longer there, not because someone stole it, but because you have exchanged it for goods and services. The money in your hand may be billions of pounds and you can keep it for millions of years, but like a dream, one day when you awake it's all gone and the rest will be history. I normally tell people that no matter how beautiful the currency note in your hand is, as long as it's money, you cannot hold it forever and it will soon fly away, like a bird beautiful in flight far above the sky.

2. MONEY IS LIKE A SPIRIT

Physically you can manipulate money, you can hold it in your hand or do what so ever you like, but money is like a spirit and spirits tend to vanish. The air inside the balloon must be maintained in order to keep it intact. Any slight mistake and the big balloon will be reduced to nothing. No one can see the wind but you can feel it. To get hold of the air you need a special method or formula and, if this is the case, the truth is you need spiritual eyes to see the money before you can be confident of making it and that is why money can be likened to a spirit.

The bible says in the book of *John 4:24 " for our God is spirit and those who must worship him must worship him in spirit and in truth.*

You need to develop your spiritual eyes adequately if you truly want to make money. People find it extremely difficult to acquire money because their spiritual eyes are blind. All they use are their physical eyes and when you look through ordinary eyes, money has limits. Do you know as you are reading this book now, somebody is already making his fortune.

There are different types of people who attend parties. Some people come to a party to enjoy themselves; they are interested in dancing, spending money, enjoy the aromatic food and exotic drinks of the night, enjoying the loud, exciting, music from the sound system and afterwards go home exhausted. There is another set of people whose interest is to make money out of the party. They still enjoy the same social benefits of the night but, after the party has finished, they are counting how much they've made from the party. The organizer of the party has spent all the money which they gathered for many months or years of labor on just for one party night. I do not say organizing a party is bad. Not at all, it's good to enjoy your money as long as you have enough to do so. My point is to draw your attention on how people see things differently.

DEVELOP YOUR INNER EYES

Some people say money is hard. Why? Because their spiritual eyes are blind. If your spiritual eyes are not opened, you cannot see available opportunities all around you. The eyes I am talking about here are not your wide open eyeballs, after all there are blind people who have not seen with their naked eyes. Yet still they are multimillionaires, for instance, Stevie Wonder the blind singer from America or Ray Charles; these are successful people even if they are blind.. Your spiritual eyes are the eyes inside, even in the midst of the deep darkness, your inner eyes will see clearly. The house that you live in now is familiar to you. You are used to your environment you have mastered every aspect of the house, even in the night you can walk round the whole place without stumbling, not because you have some strange power, but because you have developed your inner eyes. These inner eyes are also referred to as visions, dreams, imagination and ideas.

WHAT DO YOU SEE

I wrote earlier in the book about the two men who travelled to India. One of them saw the Indian people with no shoes and the other one saw how to put shoes on their feet. One of them will end up being poor and the other one successful. *Every problem you fix will determine how successful you are but you can't fix any problem until you see it with your spiritual eyes*. That's why if there is anything to develop first, it's your spiritual eyes, nothing happens physically unless our spiritual eyes are mastered first.

You didn't just get where you are today. You've started your journey a long time ago through your spirit mind. If you are not satisfied with where you are right now, then you need to start another journey and plan it properly through your inner mind. The more you develop your spiritual mind the better you start making money. Some people waste time and energy concerning themselves with things that are not productive. Others argue and discuss the issue for hours and within such a period of time, somebody is making money.

Cell phone companies are making huge amounts of money. Every time someone uses the phone it is a medium for them to acquire money. I see your life transformed by the renewing of your mind. That's why the bible says *be ye not conformed to this world but be transformed by the renewing of your mind.* There are good people around you but your mind tells you they are bad. Your mind lies to you and convinces you that everybody is a liar. Money is like a spirit, if you cannot see it you will never have it and remember money is in everything. Money is everywhere. You will only have it when your mind can comprehend it .May God help us to renew our mind.

3. MONEY IS CURRENT

Money is called currency because it flows and the money you had in your pocket last week, is probably no longer with you. It flows. Some of us see our money flying away, but we don't ask where it's flying to. The bible say - *give, and it shall be given back to you, good measure, pressed down, and shaken together, and running over, shall men give into your bosom.*

I see money flowing towards you like a river. I am not talking about your hard work; we will get there shortly. Hard work does not make you rich. It's a lie that hard work makes people rich, it kills the body. Even the bible warns us to be careful, that we should not work too hard to make money. *Please don't overwork yourself to make money.*

TITANIC - THE SHIP THAT SANK

Money is current; it will not stay in your hands indefinitely. You need to exchange it, give it for a purpose. That is why if you are giving out money you must know the reason for giving it out.

It took many great efforts to get money in your hands and remember that it has wings, it may fly away without apologies; you have to be careful so that your money doesn't flow in the wrong direction. Many people have mistakenly turned their asset into a liability; assets are things that produce you money [income]. If I may ask you what are your assets? To some, asset is strength, the only thing that brings money. Have you ever asked yourself this question; did the Titanic sink? If you remember the story the owner was so confident that the ship would never sink, he even boasted that even God could not destroy it. And what happened to the Titanic? It sank deep in the middle of the ocean and many lives were lost. In other words your strength is not a guarantee - anything can happen.

IS YOUR ASSET GREATER THAN YOUR LIABILITY?

Have you ever thought what would happen if you were sick and admitted to hospital? What would you do to make money? God forbid this should happen to anyone, but the reality is nobody ever expects the worst case scenario and accidents do and can happen. Normally your assets are supposed to overcome your liabilities. Your liabilities are the avenues that you spend your money on. Some of us have acquired assets which now become our liabilities. For instance, the most expensive car you have bought without asking yourself whether you can afford it is a liability.

Money is a current, its powerful enough to flow around and this is why everybody needs to sit down and analyze their income and expenditure. There is a need for every individual to analyze all details of their financial habits if they want to have financial freedom. Your assets are supposed to be greater than your liabilities. In other word, if you earn £1000, you are not expected to spend the whole £1000. You are supposed to channel your income to 40% by 60% rules at any time.

Firstly as a Christian, a 10% of your income is to pay tithes to your Church, if you don't have a church, then it goes to your Spiritual father - [your Mentor]. The rich people don't put their money anywhere anyhow.

Secondly, 20% goes to yourself - You may use this to treat yourself to good things of life such as food, shoes, jewelry, books, holiday etc.

The third 10% goes to your parents, this might be your relatives or the like.

More of this subject will be dealt with in the chapters ahead. However, at least 60% of your earning is supposed to be channeled towards assets, [i.e. Investments], something that brings you money at the end of the month, in case of any unpleasant situations that should occur. I see you in that category.

4. MONEY IS A DEFENSE

For wisdom is a defense as money is a defense. **Ecclesiastes 7:12**

No matter how good a house is, especially where crime and disorder exist; if there are no gates or doors to protect the house the building will be vulnerable to criminal attack and great destruction will befall the house. The same goes for countries where there is no defense strategy it will leave the people of that land open to attack. Money has the ability to defend you against all kinds of shameful activities and instead of disgrace, money can buy you honor and will lead you to higher places. No matter what your offence, with money in your pocket you can hire the best barrister in town. Some of you will remember a man called O.J. Simpson in America who committed murder against his wife, after a long trial in court, many people believed that he would go to prison for this atrocity but he hired one of the best lawyer in town and he was later exonerated. Michael Jackson was in the same situation when he was accused of child molestation he was able to settle the case out of court. I do not say anybody should commit crime expecting money to buy a favorable judgment but I am giving examples of the extent of power money has. Money will build an edge around you in time of trouble and assist you to get through the toughest part of life. In time of sickness money will help you obtain the best medical help available. With money you can live in the best houses and acquire all the best things of life.

Money will help you to send your children to the best schools and help to secure their future. Money will defend you against enemy attack and secure you a better place, where you can shelter away from any plans of the evil. If you have money you can speak for yourself in any circumstances, any place, anywhere. Money will shield you against any unwanted matter; money will help you to build a fence against unwanted situations.

5. MONEY WILL DRAW PEOPLE TO YOU

Wealth makes many friends, But the poor is separated from his friend Prov.19:4}

Money has a special magnet that attracts people to your life, with money in your pocket the whole world is in your hand. Everybody wants to associate with you and support you in every way they can. He that has money will definitely have many friends and all your relatives will forever surround you at all time because they can count on you for support in time of need. Money is a way of earning peoples respect, if you have money people will tolerate your behavior and accept you for who you are. Life can become interesting and enjoyable, with money you can buy all your desirable needs and meet life's expectations. You can pay for holidays of your choice and put smiles in people's faces, you can organize parties of your choice and invite as many dignitaries in society to celebrate with you. When you have money, people will always want to be around you. Money will even turn your enemies into friends. When you have money you will always have people wanting to be your friend and not your enemy.

How many people will want to be a poor man's friend? Money draws people to you. How do you know your true friends? Tell them you are going through some hardship - money wise! And ask if they can help you out financially. You will be treated to a series of excuses.

Why are poor people lonely? Because they don't have friends? No, it is because there is no money in the pocket.

People who have money are never boring, they acquire stunning life styles and the more money you have, the number of friends also increases.

When you are rich many more business opportunities will be offered to you, people will go many miles for you and many will give you gifts of all kinds, you are treated like a king, people will adore you and even worship you like God (please never allow this when you come into money, promise me now.) I see God connecting you.

6. MONEY IS USED TO FULFILL YOUR VISION: JOEL 2:28

Take a look at the air craft that flies in the sky with its many facilities. Pilot controlling the movement of the machine, cabin crew serving the nicest choice of your breakfast, the music blasting out of the sound system through earphones, sky television playing movies through the flat TV screen throughout your entire journey, all these amazing luxuries are a product of someone's God given vision. What about the ship that sails in deep oceans, providing all manner of entertainment for people, some cruises even accommodate people a month or more, providing them with a holiday of a lifetime.

There are many visions on our planet which are wonderful, revelations of somebody with an idea who turned it into reality and this would not be possible without money. ***Money is a tool that will help you to bring your vision from a common thought to reality***. If there is money, any vision can become a reality, it just depends on what you wish and desire.

I am a visionary myself and know what I went through to achieve my God given vision. When I began my journey to try and make my vision a reality, most people didn't want to help, despite my desire to help the less privileged and charity purposes. Many people I called to help me, demanded money from me even when what they had to offer would be for the benefit of our faith and to promote Christianity. I remember a particular musician who I invited to come and sing in one of the charity programmes organized to encourage people to come to church, especially those with drug -related issues. The musician refused to come, giving many excuses only because there was no money involved ***Money will guarantee you in all other supports to bring your vision to the level of supernatural.***

Money helps one to facilitate one's dream into becoming a reality. It helps to carry out one's vision. Do you know your dreams? Why are they not coming into reality at this stage? It's because you are still waiting for Money. Money is one of the tools that will help you to translate your vision. You don't need a big explanation or project-writing, when money is available because Money Talks.

Your dream will not die, God will give you money to facilitate that vision. Amen.

7. ANOINTING WITHOUT MONEY IS EQUAL TO ANNOYANCE

To be anointed means you are doing what you know best without struggling or you are fulfilling your God given assignment. The ability to do things without fighting means you are anointed, for instance some people can sing melodiously, yet they find it difficult to dance or play musical instrument. Some people can accomplish the most delicate things in life but cannot handle the simplest situation; this is called anointing.

My point is that no matter how well you handle your vision, with the help of money you can take your vision to another level. What good is a qualified driver with excellent driving skills if he has no money to buy a car. What use is a carpenter who knows how to handle professional equipment if he has no money to buy such equipment. These obstacles lead to anger and frustration.

MONEY WILL TAKE YOU TO ANOTHER LEVEL

No matter what you can do, with money you are likely to take anything to another level, nobody wants to stay in the same position doing the same thing over and over again, there will always be room for improvement in all professions and this can only be possible with money. There was a particular time in my life when, having been involved in video production for many years, recording all kinds of occasions, weddings, christenings, dramas, concerts etc.

I decided to go to the School of Filming, where I would learn to produce, direct and become a cinematographer .

I got in contact with PANICO a professional school in London, where I was told the cost of studying would be over £10,000. I could not do anything apart from wait until I had money to implement my ambition. This is the point I am making. Even the fact that you are gifted and have something special, if there is no money to improve yourself all you will achieve is a sense of frustration and this is one of the reasons why some people commit suicide. Everyone wants to do better in their profession and the best way to do this is in conjunction with money.

There are musicians who are extremely talented but have been unable to use a recording studio because they do not have the money. When you cannot achieve your best, you will definitely get angry. I see God transforming your life, giving you more than enough to help you out from any helpless situation.

8. MONEY IS IN EVERYTHING AND MONEY IS EVERY

Whenever people say I have no money, what they are actually saying is that they lack ideas that produce money, no body lacks money, what they lack is the medium of exchange for the money. Money is a legal tender, just a piece of paper printed for the exchange of goods and services.

Whatever you do, money is always part of the equation, however great or small. There is money in everything and money is everywhere. You just need to develop the mind-set of acquiring the money. If someone asked you for a certain amount of money, even when there is no money in your pocket please never says 'I don't have any money" you might be being honest but the reality is that with this statement you have closed your mind by giving a negative response. All possibilities of making any money will be taken away from you, both spiritually or physically.

MONEY IS IN YOUR DISCOVERY

Instead of responding negatively, try a positive response. "Presently I have no cash with me, give me some time I will get back to you", with this kind of statement you can now open your mind and listen to your heart. The law of attraction will help you to channel that money towards you, it will happen as long as your mind is open and not closed.

We will explore this further in other chapters, what I am pointing out is that money is in everything you only need to open your eyes wide and use wisdom to get the money. For example, if you can make people laugh, all you have to do is start a comedy show. If you can have a certain figure, you can become a model, and if you know how to dance and sing you can become a professional entertainer. If you have the skill of teaching people, you can become a teacher.

Everybody on earth is created to do something; all you need is to discover this for yourself and act on it, *what so ever you know how to do, there is money attached, you only need the wisdom to make money out of your discovery.*

There is no place where money is not required in one way or the others. Even rubbish and smelling drainage requires money to get rid of it.

You should realize the fact that everything around you involves money! What you lack is the ability to make it. Everyone needs money. Money is in everything. Money is everywhere.

9. MONEY WILL ANSWER ALL THINGS - Eccles. 10:19

A man was once complimented on the beauty of his wife, how impeccably she dressed and how elegant and charming she was. The man responded with another question "Why is your own wife so ugly and not dressed immaculately especially at social occasions?" The man with the ugly wife laughed and said "You know my problem is I have no money to buy all the luxuries for my wife". The other man apologized and explained that every woman is beautiful as long as there is money, **_with money in your pocket you can turn the most ugly things in life into the world of beauty._** If you ever notice something around you which is not looking right just let money show up, the situation will be resolved immediately.

You might not be where you would like to be right now. I tell you it's just a matter of time when money touches your hand all your questions about life will be answered. No matter what your opinion is about this statement, the word of God is settled and there is no controversy about it. Money answers all things, including spiritual life, **_you may not buy your salvation but you need money to buy the ingredient that surrounds your salvation_**,

To be sound you need money to buy good teaching books, CDs, DVDs and all other Christian's literatures. For good evangelism and to expand the gospel further you need money. Money will take your ministry to another level. Do you want to be on the national television and preaching the gospel or you like to feed the homeless and help the needy? Money will answer these questions.

The bigger the dream in your life, the greater the vision that is in your mind. Money will give you an answer. There are great things you may wish to do, holiday you love to go, education you wish to further, improvement of your health and many more Money will definitely answer all these things.

10. WISDOM GATHERS MONEY AND FOOLISHNESS CASTS IT AWAY!

The more wisdom you derive the better money you will acquire. Money comes when your eyes are open wide to see opportunities and you can quickly make use of them. Foolishness, on the other hand, will help you to lose your money. There are many areas in our life that we ignorantly neglect; we refuse to pay special attention to and in the end we lose out. Many people could have acquired millions but because of foolishness they lost the golden opportunity. Foolishness works alongside wisdom and the wisdom you use in the wrong side of your brain will be the foolishness that slaps you on your face without an apology. The reason I say this is that most people do not know that they operate in the field of foolishness, believing they are very clever and wise in their own eyes. Nobody wants to make a foolish mistake, everybody wants to be perfect, but things do go wrong when we make a wrong decision. Sometimes we pay attention and sometimes we ignore our inner mind. We can learn from other people's experiences or ignore them.

As far as human beings are concerned, nobody likes to be foolish, unfortunately not all people are wise, it all depends on how we individually use our brain, right or wrong, everybody can subscribe to his own opinion.

Have you seen some rich people who are broke and became poor as if they have never tasted money before. They started very well, everybody recognized them in society, and they worked hard to attain their greatness. Before you know what happens, they have dropped from number one to number ten in the top ten richest people list. Suddenly they are forgotten, like flowers that arose in the morning and in the evening they faded away. The problem with such people cannot be accounted to anything other than foolishness. To gather money can take years but foolishness will disperse money within seconds. If you don't make use of wisdom, foolishness will show up. Life is full of both. Make use of wisdom you will see that money comes to you without struggling.

BE CAREFUL OF THE MOUSE

There was this story about two rich men, one was wise and other was foolish. The wise man, after acquiring much money, took it to the bank and invested the money which produced even more money. The foolish rich man was afraid and never trusted anybody. He made a decision to keep the money in his own house by locking it inside the cupboard. After a while he went back to check on the money, only to realize all the money had been eating up by a mouse. You may not keep your money in the mouse cupboard but your mind is the cupboard of your life *what so ever you do right in the corner of your mind will determine the result of your life.*

According to the bible Wisdom is the principal thing. The bridge between the rich and the poor is wisdom. The lesson from this story is that one is able to use his common sense while the other did not. One is spending his money on rubbish while the other is investing it. Always be careful of every decision you make in life.

THE SUMMARY OF THE
TRUTH ABOUT MONEY

- THE MORE TRUTH YOU KNOW THE BETTER YOU PERFORM AND YOUR CONFIDENCE WILL INCREASE.
- ONLY THE TRUTH CAN CREATE A GOOD IMPACT IN OUR LIFE.

SOME TRUTHS ABOUT MONEY

1. MONEY HAS WINGS. IT CAN FLY AWAY. - *PRO.23:5*
2. MONEY IS LIKE A SPIRIT. – *ECCL. 8:8*
   YOU NEED BOTH EYES TO SEE IT.
3. MONEY IS A CURRENT - IT FLOWS *LUKE 6:38*
4. MONEY IS A DEFENSE *ECCL. 7:12*
5. MONEY DRAWS PEOPLE CLOSER TO YOUR LIFE -*PRO.19:4*
6. MONEY HELPS TO FACILITATE YOUR VISION.
7. ANOINTING WITHOUT MONEY WILL LEAD TO ANNOYANCE
8. MONEY IS IN EVERYTHING AND MONEY IS EVERYWHERE
9. MONEY IS THE ANSWER TO ALL THINGS *ECCL.10:19*
10. WISDOM GATHERS MONEY - FOOLISHNESS CASTS IT AWAY
    PRO.9 :1

CHAPTER FIVE
TEN WAYS OF MAKING MONEY

If you can count your money, you don't have a billion dollars.
J. Paul Getty (1892 - 1976)

*The righteous shall flourish like a palm tree; He shall grow like a cedar in Lebanon. those who are planted in the house of the LORD Shall flourish in the courts of our God they shall still bear fruit in old age; they shall be fresh and flourishing, To declare that the LORD is upright; He is my rock, and there is no unrighteousness in Him. **Psalm. 92:12-15.***

Fundamentally money is everywhere. The problem is that the majority of people are blind spiritually (lack of vision). They have the natural eyes but they have no power to see all the chances available around them to make money. What you cannot see, you cannot acquire! It's God desire for man to operate to his full potential as long as he is still on this earth, every one of us is fully equipped with great benefit, according to the scripture God said "Let us make man in our own image "and He blessed them saying "Be fruitful and multiply."- *Gen.1:26 -28*.

Psalm 68:19 "for God loaded us with daily benefit" -you are not just an ordinary person who exists for the sake of existing. . The whole of God head lives inside of you. Every man can be whatever he inspires to be; you are created with the mind of God. You need no government benefit or anyone to survive because you are fully loaded and capable to succeed in life on your own; every facility needed to survive is in you. God gave you eyes to see, a mind to think, ears to hear and a mouth to speak. The bible says "you *will decree a thing and it shall come to past*".

You have the right to determine for yourself how wealthy you want to be. If you want you can reach the level of a millionaire or a billionaire, or you can decide to be the richest person ever to live on this planet.

DECIDE YOUR OWN LEVEL

There are five categories of people living in the world performing differently on the level of their financial status:

1. The poor [the most common of all], this set of people are the lowest of all in society. They depend on other people to survive The life of a poor man is full of sorrow and pain, everything is very difficult, they have no say in the community because no amount of ideas a poor person may have cannot be taken seriously even if the ideas are very wonderful. Poverty is not a crime but dying poor is shameful.

2. The rich

These are the people who taking over the affairs of the society, to be rich means you have enough capital and you are financially capable. The rich are measured by the money they have in their account, they have money they can use to achieve their goals in life, people are always ready to befriend anyone who is rich, and their voices can always be heard in the community. Everybody wants to be rich, they like to take holidays of their choice, live in mansions and do extraordinary things in life. Some people will do anything to be in this place as they want to get out of poverty and be financially free. That is why they do enough work which will bring them riches but remember do not overwork yourself to be rich.

3. The wealthy

This group is well above the rich. The rich can only account for the cash whilst to be wealthy is synonymous with both cash and assets. These are business minded people. They have many investments all over. They are financially educated and can help others to be rich. Wealthy people are not afraid of poverty because they have more than enough. They have a lot of collateral which they can use as security when they need to borrow from the bank. Wealthy people are investors, they sit on many company boards as director or adviser. If you are wealthy, everybody wants to know you and build a strong relationship with you. I call wealthy people the power point of life; they have investments in land, companies, houses, resources and much more. Many people have tried hard to get to this level and because of the great effort involved, a lot of people hang on to this position and refuse to move to the next level. I called this level the financial comfort zone, but there is still another higher level to be attained. After all you did not arrive here on your own, the bible says *"I am the Lord that gives you power to make wealth"*.

4. The Prosperous - (Gen.26:12-13)

To be prosperous means you are a great success in all areas of life. You have acquired more than enough; you are both wealthy and successful.

Prosperous people are financially sound and they do not have to struggle to pay for expenses. They have glorious investments all around the globe; prosperous people are masters of business with all different kinds of experience. When you are in this category you are confident and capable of dealing with any business at any level; you do not need to borrow from the bank anymore because banks are looking up to you as financier and the government of the land cannot overlook you in times of financial decisions. Every wealthy person is in the reach of a prosperous status. Immediately you arrive in the place of prosperity you are rest assured that you will never be poor in life again because you are blessed and highly favored by God A prosperous man will leave inheritance for his children till at least the fourth generation. Many people can't attain this level due to ungodliness. If you live a clean life and avoid what will place you on a curse you will definitely prosper according to *Psalm 1:1-4.* If you are praying for prosperity, you are only limiting your level.

5. *The Flourishing*

This is the highest level of success in the world. People who are in this criteria have everything in abundance. They live comfortable lifestyles and are well respected in society. This is the level God wants for all his children and that is why *Matt. 6:33* says " seek ye first the kingdom of God and His righteousness every other thing shall be added" people who are kingdom minded will live a righteous life and only a righteous man can flourish, everything about you is productive, nothing is wasted. All things connected to your life have something to reproduce, your words, ideas, philosophy everything. If you are flourishing, you are more than average, above the rich and the wealthy and the prosperous.

BE LIKE A PALM TREE

There are many available channels to make money, but unfortunately many do concentrate on one area, forgetting that accidents do happen. Being flourishing means you don't have to struggle for any things in your life anymore. Everything about you increases, people at this stage just call out for money whenever they need it, and behold money goes to them as much as they want.

This set of people have made their name, they have created a niche for themselves. When their names are imprinted on products, such products attain a 'sell-out' level. When you invite flourishing people to a programme, such an event becomes a hit because of the caliber of people involved.

Why would the bible qualify us to be a "*palm tree*"? Try and analyze a palm tree. It grows in tropical land such as in Jamaica and Africa where the sun always shine.

THESE ARE THE TEN CHANNELS OF ACQUIRING MONEY

God has given every one of us the best abilities in life which are to equip us for success. The more you discover the area of interest the better you perform, however some of us have ignored certain parts and that is why some people cannot function well. Life can only get better by educating and positioning yourself. The ten channels below will determine how quickly you benefit, the earlier you make use of these channels the quicker you can derive the level of your financial stand in life and my prayer is that God will open your eyes of understanding.

CHANNEL ONE:

WORK OR EMPLOYMENT

This is the most common and traditional way on which everybody in society knows how to acquire money. According to **2 Thessalonians 3:10 says "For even when we were with you, we commanded you this: If anyone will not work, neither shall he eat.**

Right from the foundation of the world, men are known to be the working force of the earth. To work means to take an employment where money is paid for the exchange of your labor and time. By working, you are capable of acquiring money depending on the type of work you do. It could either be a menial job such as cleaning, laborer etc. or a professional job such as doctor, solicitor, pilot, teacher etc. When you work you exercise your body system and it helps you to take care of your leisure and social needs, and also takes care of your family needs. You are free from depending on others financially. The bible says - "we do not depend on you for our money, we work day and night". It's never a criminal offence to work, in whatever field we might be trained for, be it carpentry, plumbing, banking, accounting, and nursing. It is a legitimate channel for making money.

YOU CAN'T PARK HERE

Work or employment is one of the main ways of acquiring money and this channel is where the general population of the world remain, hoping that they can be rich and successful in life. Although this channel is only an entry form, it's just a stepping stone to getting to your desired level. Unfortunately most people rest on this avenue for a life time, what a mistake. If I may ask you how much have you got from your years of employment? Please ponder over it. Do you ever think that your present employment is able to sustain you forever? The maximum period you can work for a company is 65 years of age. This depends on the individual countries employment law. Get this understanding; any income from your work is just to cater for your daily needs as in food, shelter [rent], pay bills, pay tax so that the Government can keep its budget up. This system is referred to as the rat race, wake up go to work, come back and keep doing the same thing all over again. Your life should not keep repeating itself. To acquire more money you need more than this system and as I said earlier, it's just a foundation which everybody needs in this life.

THE MOST COMMON MISTAKE

In the age of technology and the modern world, more people are now working round the clock, the night is indistinguishable from day as the streets are filled with people going to work or retuning from jobs. Some people are working both day or night towards the goal of making money. People are taking on extra jobs to meet with demand and some people have gone as far as doing overtime because they want to be successful.

Proverb 23:4- Do not overwork to be rich.

The bible says, for your own good, stop this now. The danger is that you are destroying your body bit-by-bit, if care is not taken. Overtime can destroy families, as people give less time to their children, their spouses or themselves. The crime rate today is increasing due to this factor, let's face it, even normal work doesn't make you rich, how do you think overtime will make you rich? Some will even go as far to exchange their resting period or holiday for overtime work, what a mistake. Some Christians could not worship their God even on Sundays because of over time. Never spend all your energy in this channel, it's time to wake up, you are living in a competitive world, you deserve the best, seek another level. After all life is full of many stages and you are bound to take one step after the others.

Never overspend your energy in that same job over a long period of time whilst there are other avenues available to you.

CHANNEL TWO:

BUSINESS OR INVESTMENT

There are different kinds of businesses such as trading, buying and selling goods or services. Business provides the ability to sell for the purpose of profit making; this could be in the form of sole trader, partnership, venture, factory or establishment in any form for the benefit of making money. A good business will connect you to many opportunities, The mistake that people make is that they think you need money to own your business. The truth is that what you need first is the business idea in your mind and proper plan to go with it. Although nobody would argue that money produces a better business deal, money isn't necessary to start all business, it all depends on what kinds of business you have in mind. Society has taught us the philosophy of money in order to enter the world of business, due to this everybody in society is working hard to gather money hoping to start their own business one day and in this process many people never enter the world of business. To start your business is not as difficult as you think; the majority of business people started their business with little or no money. I have done it myself, building my business without any money. If you like more information regarding this, my book is available to buy titled GRAB YOUR OPPORTUNITY. In that book I explained fully the details about this topic and many testimonies on how to start your business without hassles.

Among the people on the earth the Chinese people are the major users of this channel. Whenever they travel to other countries, instead of looking for work, they look for business opportunities and that is why many of the Chinese are millionaires.

ENTERING THE WORLD OF INVESTIMENT

Investment is putting money into something with the expectation of profit. More specifically, investment is the commitment of money or capital to the purchase of financial and there are different types of investments such as the following :

LEVERAGE.

This is the degree to which an investor or business utilizes borrowed money. Companies that are highly leveraged may be at risk of bankruptcy if they are unable to make payments on their debt; they may also be unable to find new lenders in the future.

Leverage is not always bad; it can increase the shareholders' return on their investment and often there are tax advantages associated with borrowing. It can also be referred to as O.P.M. which means other people's money Are you aware that millionaires live on other people's money?

Most especially in Europe, you can only buy a property through a mortgage system The company will lend you large sums money and you pay this back in monthly installments. Many people have taken advantage of this system. For instance, people who acquire a council property after long tenancy, they bought the house from the government and later sold it or re-mortgaged the property and used the equity to climb up onto the property ladder. Through this system a lot of people are now very rich and live a comfortable life.

PRECIOUS METALS AND PRECIOUS GEMS

Precious stones are categorized as diamond, ruby, sapphire and emerald, with all other gemstones being semi-precious. Gold has been sought after for its inimitable blend of near indestructibility, beauty, rarity and because of its status as a means of exchange it has been a universal currency par excellence for centuries. Many people have sought to possess gold as a medium of international exchange, as a store of wealth in order to increase and preserve power. Individuals have used gold as an insurance against the fluctuations and depreciation of paper money.

Successful investing is about the diversification and management of risk. In layman's terms this means not having all your eggs in one basket.

We know from history that markets do crash and if you are not properly diversified, your nest egg can be severely affected. Gold, silver and platinum are the best-known precious metals. Silver is often seen as a more volatile play on gold, while platinum has a wide range of uses in industry.

MONEY MARKET

The money market consists of financial institutions and dealers in money or credit for those who wish to either borrow or lend. Participants borrow and lend for short periods of time, typically up to thirteen months. Money market trades in short-term financial instruments commonly called "paper." This contrasts with the capital market for longer-term funding, which is supplied by bonds and equity.

The core of the money market consists of banks borrowing and lending to each other, using commercial paper, repurchase agreements and similar instruments. These instruments are often benchmarked to (i.e. priced by reference to) the London Interbank Offered Rate (LIBOR) for the appropriate term and currency.

RETIREMENT FUND

In general, a **pension** is an arrangement to provide people with an income when they are no longer earning a regular income from employment.

STOCK MARKET

A **stock market** or **equity market** is a public market (a loose network of economic transactions, not a physical facility or discrete entity) for the trading of company stock (shares) and derivatives at an agreed price; these are securities listed on a stock exchange as well as those only traded privately. The size of the world stock market was estimated at about $36.6 trillion USD at the beginning of October2008 the *total* world derivatives market has been estimated at about $791 trillion face or nominal value, 11 times the size of the entire world economy. Participants in the stock market range from small individual stock investors to large hedge fund traders, who can be based anywhere. Their orders usually end up with a professional at a stock exchange, who executes the order.

TREASURY BILL

A short-term debt obligation backed by the U.S. government with a maturity of less than one year. T-bills are sold in denominations of $1,000 up to a maximum purchase of $5 million and commonly have maturities of one month (four weeks), three months (13 weeks) or six months (26 weeks). T-bills are issued through a competitive bidding process at a discount from par, this means that rather than paying fixed interest payments like conventional bonds, the appreciation of the bond provides the return to the holder.

Investopedia explains *Treasury Bill - T-Bill*. For example, let's say you buy a 13-week T-bill priced at $9,800. Essentially, the U.S. government (and its nearly bullet proof credit rating) writes you an IOU for $10,000 that it agrees to pay back in three months.

You will not receive regular payments as you would with a coupon bond, for example. Instead, the appreciation - and, therefore, the value to you - comes from the difference between the discounted value you originally paid and the amount you receive back ($10,000). In this case, the T-bill pays a 2.04% interest rate ($200/$9,800 = 2.04%) over a three month period.

COMMODITY MARKET

This is where raw or primary products are exchanged. These raw commodities are traded on regulated commodities exchanges, in which they are bought and sold in standardized contracts.

Historically, dating from ancient Sumerian use of sheep or goats, other people used pigs, rare seashells, or other items as commodity money, people have sought ways to standardize and trade contracts in the delivery of such items, to render trade itself more smooth and predictable.

REAL ESTATE.

is a legal term (in some jurisdictions, such as the United Kingdom, Canada, Australia, USA and the Bahamas) that encompasses land along with improvements to the land, buildings, fences, wells and other site improvements that are fixed in location—immovable

In most advanced economies, the main source of capital used by individuals and small companies to purchase and improve land and buildings is mortgage loans (or other instruments). These are loans for which the real property itself constitutes collateral. Banks are willing to make such loans at rates in large part because, if the borrower does not make payments, the lender can foreclose by filing a court action which allows them to take back the property and sell it to get their money back. For investors, profitability can be enhanced by using a plan or pre-construction strategy to purchase at a lower price, which is often the case in the pre-construction phase of development.

These are some of the investments available, more information can be found from any investment advisor, you only need to enquire to know which investment will suit you. If you are serious about making money just step out and seek counseling as the bible recorded *"For by wise counsel you wage your own war, and in the multitude of counselors there is safety* - **Proverbs 24:6**

In whatsoever you invest in, please make sure you invest wisely and be smart, always make use of expert advice.

There are downward investments, something you put your money on which does not yield an increase, and upward investments, something which produces an increase and adds more value. Making use of this channel will guarantee you more money and great opportunity to meet up with your needs in life. This is the anchor to the remaining channel, when you are business minded or good a investor you are rest assure that you can acquire you desirable money in life.

CHANNEL THREE:

(N.B.T) NATURAL BORN TALENT

Everyone is born with a natural gift without any exception, the purpose for this gift is to help individuals to acquire greatness in life and also help them fulfill every assignment God has given. We are all on assignment, you are born to fulfill certain obligation in life. Heaven knows there are obstacles which can destroy peoples' destiny, which is why people are born to solve certain problems. Let me put it this way, tailors are born to solve the problem of nudity, comedians are born to make you laugh, musicians are born to solve the problem of entertainment. Every gifted person on earth is placed there to solve one problem or another and that is why I said earlier that money is in the problem you can solve.

When you have an NBT, it's another way of making money but you need to discover your own gift.

DISCOVER YOUR TALENT

Many people are gifted in various ways, yet because of much distraction, they are struggling to know who they are. The more you refuse to discover your natural born talent, the more you are losing out in the financial world. In the world of golf, Tiger Wood was discovered. In formula one, Lewis Hamilton became a household name and thank God for football. David Beckham will never be forgotten. In the world of the boxing generation we all remember people like Mohamed Ali and many others in different categories, be it fashion, sport, medical, religious, music, media etc.

All these people used their natural talent to acquire lots of money and today history will never forget them, none of them are better than you. They are all ordinary people who did extra ordinary things and were successful. The greatest secret is that they discovered themselves.

The bible says "the *gift of man will make room for him*" your gift will pave the way for you anywhere, anytime, when you are naturally gifted people will know you and associate with you and your gift will bring you great fortune.

As a musician myself, I have enjoyed great opportunities with all sorts of people in society, from the common man to people of high authority. I do not need to travel anywhere with money in my pocket as just a single concert will bring me enough money for my journey. Really and truly it pays to enter in to the world of your gift.

HOW TO DISCOVER YOURSELF

Everybody is gifted in their own way, there is no doubt about it, you only need to discover yours. There are different means to achieve this, below are ways in which to discover your own gifts or natural born talents.

Firstly, whatever you do with ease, without struggling is your natural talent. Some people find it extremely difficult to do certain things which takes them ages and wastes their time. What takes others ages can only take some a few days to achieve and everybody wonders how did they managed it? That is your natural born talent.

Secondly, there are certain things that occupy your mind, this is where you constantly have an idea in your mind and in your heart, sometimes you wish to avoid the scenario to concentrate on other things, but the idea is constantly a priority in you thinking, that something is your God given talent, just pay attention to it. The majority of all the wondrous things that exist in our planet today started just like that. Inventions such as computers, electricity, machinery, science and technology automobiles etc. is a result of priority thinking. Any idea that dominates your thinking all the time is what can be defined as your talent.

Thirdly, other people's opinions are very important. If more than one person is complimenting you on a certain talent you possess, it might be worth paying attention to what people say about you. Each time you are complimented on something special you have achieved, it may be because that is your talent. The majority of people you see today were actually discovered by somebody else, if you move with the right people who know you better than yourself, they will help you to know who you are and what assignment you are to fulfill on earth. I have heard of people who did not think they had anything special to offer until someone helped them out and today these people are great and well-known in this society. Please, if you have not discovered yourself, start listening to good things people around you are saying, this is where your natural gift lies.

Fourthly, there are pains in your heart which make you uncomfortable, most especially when you notice how people around you are achieving their goals, with little or no talent. There is this inner voice which keeps saying, you can do better than that even though what is going on has nothing to do with you. For example, you are invited by a friend to a party and inside the party you notice the way the organizer is doing things and it's not right. Everything is just falling apart, there is no proper planning, everything seems upside down yet all the invited guests are enjoying their party without noticing all of these mistakes except you. The fact that you've noticed these details and know that you could achieve better results, shows that this may be the assignment and talent that you need to discover and this is where your money can be made.

There is more money to be made in a natural born talent than any other areas of life, you only need to discover yourself and whatever you know, please do take it to another level.

A STORY OF A SISTER AND A GENTLEMAN

There was a sister who came out of drugs, prostitution, and a prison sentence; she decided to look for employment but all in vain and, after much searching, she lost all hope of finding a job. I invited her to my office one day to have a talk. In the middle of counseling I asked her what was her natural talent, she told me she had none. I pressed further asking her if she could tell me anything she was good at. She told me she liked creating things with her hands; hairdressing was a particular activity she enjoyed and was quite good at. I advised her and encouraged her to start something using her hands, today the lady in question is making money as a talented hairdresser.

Another young man also came to me one day and complained of not having a job and many times he had tried without any luck. I also gave him counseling and found out he was quite informed about building works. The gentleman in question presently is acquiring a lot of money and also employs many others to work for him.

CHANNEL FOUR:

WISDOM.

If you have wisdom, you've got everything. The bible says *"Wisdom is the principal thing" Proverb 4:7-9*

To acquire money is not by power or strength. Anything you do in this life if you don't apply **wisdom**, it is doomed for failure. Wisdom will empower you, where others fail you will be successful. Life is full of opportunities; only wisdom will grant you the sovereignty to know the better way, in the midst of wisdom greatness is guaranteed. Wisdom will single you out of the crowd; any one with wisdom will surely lead the way. Everything that stays on the surface of our planet is put together by wisdom, the government system, traffic system, building, aviation, utilities just to mention a few of them. Everything's made possible with the help of wisdom and whenever you can make use of wisdom, automatically money will roll in.

WISDOM WILL HELP YOU TO BUILD

I started my business called Communication Link without a penny.

How? The idea came to me after being sacked from my formal employment some time ago. I was determined to create a job for myself, having decided on the name and what exactly to do. I had money only to rent an office, of which I did. After renting the office I was left with nothing and did not know how to raise any more money. God dropped a thought into my mind. The thought was to write a signboard and I had to look for a sign-writer who demanded £470. I was very angry with myself for not being able to raise the money, not knowing that I could sign-write myself by way of my profession as a fine artiste. Do you know that when a problem arises, we are so preoccupied with the problem, the solution is very often staring us in the face.

This is why people make mistakes in life; this is why people need to renew their mind and look for the obvious. With £5, I bought all the materials such as pencil, ruler, paint, etc. that I would need for the sign-board of my proposed business. Whilst working on the sign-board, people started asking if I was a sign-writer, which I answered in the affirmative. Before I knew what was happening, I started getting contracts and raised money for my proposed business.

So what you need is not money to start a business, as I have said earlier on, but wisdom. Wisdom is in everything and wisdom is everywhere. Remember the bible says money is a defense, as wisdom is also a defense. Wisdom is the ability to apply common sense and the more you know how to apply wisdom in everything the more you acquire money. ***Remember nobody has a problem of money what they lack is wisdom to make money.***

CHANNEL FIVE:

DIVINE IDEAS

These are things God reveals to people in their dreams or visions, these are supernatural revelations that are revealed to you sometimes, somewhere in your environment. What happens to those dreams? Some of you get inspirational advice in your dreams. What has happened to those great dreams/visions? You have not made use of them, do you know that those things you received from your dreams can help you to acquire money if you can take advantage.

For instance, the public address system (PA) that blast the sound and microphone being used in conference didn't just sprung up out the blue; someone got the inspirational/divine knowledge and turned it into Money.

When God reveals things to you in your dreams, please don't let them die. Martin Luther King who is popularly known for his saying *"I have a dream"* got this revelation many years ago and today after 45years, that vision is a reality.

GREAT IDEAS PRODUCE GREAT MONEY

Money is in your vision/dream, God reveals great ideas to most people but they refuse to act on it. You need to work on your own vision or idea, the ability to come out with your original idea will place you in Guinness Book of World Records, you will be celebrated and gain more popularity and connect you with great people. Everybody has different ways of doing things and whatever is your idea, it is yours. If you work on your vision money will never be far away from you. I see your visions coming to pass in Jesus' name. Someone is waiting to buy your imaginative inventions. So begin to imagine new things. For instant, when Barclays realized that slavery was going to be abolished, he began to think of how to better still enslave people, Barclays Bank idea was established, and today almost everybody is enslaved to Barclays Bank in form of Loans, Credit cards, etc. Whatever the ideas in your mind, you can start making money and possess a better future, after all freely have you been given by God.

CHANNEL SIX:

INHERITANCE

This is a will left behind for people either from their parents, relatives, neighbor or even strangers. Sometimes life may be unfair but there are many surprises, you only need to keep your eyes wide open and do good to all that come your way, as you never know who can reward you in life. the bible says in the book of **Acts 10:38** "*how God anointed Jesus of Nazareth with the Holy Spirit and power who went about doing good and healing all who were oppressed by the devil for God was with him*".

THE REWARD OF SOUL WINNING

I remember a story of an evangelist who was a pastor at a church in America. He had a passion for soul winning and God used him mightily in the areas of drugs, prostitution, alcohol and all kinds of aggressive youth behavior. The Lord was really using this man to convert people to Christianity and there was one particular young boy who this man led to the Lord and the boy's life changed tremendously from crack to Christ.

One day, after a mid-week service, the pastor settled back in his office and offered a thanksgiving prayer to the Lord. Immediately as he opened his eyes, a man walked in unannounced and asked aggressively "Are you the pastor who changed my son's life?" The pastor was stammering, with confusion in his eyes, as he did not know the intention behind this aggressive question. The man could not even wait for the pastor's answer before he said he will be back shortly.

The tension of the pastor and the other brothers with the man of God was very high and everybody was speechless, they were all afraid and were still deciding what to do when the man walked back in with a handshake and said thank you for changing my son's life. The man gave the pastor an envelope which he opened. The white envelope contained a million dollar cheque and that was the way this God fearing man became a millionaire and his ministry transformed completely. Your father may not be a millionaire or be able to leave an inheritance for you, but nobody can tell what the Lord has in store for you. My advice is keep on doing the good you know how to do best, one day some body may include you in their inheritance.

Money is not the only thing you can inherit, some families have plenty of land which can be exchanged for money, and some have properties, family business, treasure, ancient valuable materials or even ordinary names *"good name is better than silver or gold"* what so ever is it, there is money in inheritance.

Have this in your mind, money may be the handwork of man, but man never owns money. God owns money, just like He owns everything on earth. Your Father in heaven is more than a billionaire; He is ready to make you an heir to all His wealth only if you get closer to Him.

CHANNEL SEVEN:

FORTUNE OR LUCK

(This is not a recommendation from me but it is still a way of making money.)

One day as I tuned in to the sky digital television to watch my normal evening news, all of sudden some people gathered together with a video camera and some heavy flash photograph cameras. As I looked further, two couples in their 40s were being celebrated on the channel and a cheque of £50 million was handed over to them. To my surprise the chairman of Camelot came forward to announce that the couple had won one of the biggest jackpots in Europe, what an amazing story. Many people are making huge amounts of money from good fortune which can also be referred to as luck, although as a Christian there is nothing called luck, instead you are blessed and highly favored. Every day in Europe the grocery shop is full of people lining up to buy lottery tickets, people go to William Hill to gamble and money comes to them easily. Some walk in empty handed but come out with a fat cheque, don't get me wrong I do not encourage anyone to use this medium to make money as a Christian, but, fair enough those who are not of the faith will definitely find pleasure in acquiring money in those sorts of places. Apart from gambling, some people pick money from the floor and become successful through this as well.

MONEY IN THE GALLON

I heard an amazing story which actually shocked my belief system.

This is a true story and it all happened in Lagos City in Nigeria some time ago. A certain poor man, who rented a single room, was praying and petitioning God to do something about his financial situation. Not long after he finished his prayers, he heard a sound of rain and decided to go and collect the rainfall. As he was rolling the gallon barrel to the main pole where the rain would fall directly into the container, the man noticed a strange object that looked like a sack. He pulled it out and opened the bag only for him to realize the bag was full of money. Just like a dream, he closed the bag immediately and quickly took it inside his room to show his wife. Both of them were speechless and conspired to hide the money and wait to see if anyone announced the loss of a bag.

After a while, news came on the television about some armed robbers who were engaged in criminal activity very nearby close to the poor man's street and in the process of the crime the police killed some of them and arrested some who later confessed their part in the evil plot. Meanwhile, the poor man was afraid to go to the police as this could endanger his own life due to the corrupt system in the country. When still nobody had declared the loss of the bag, after a long period of time the man took the money to the bank and later started a business which made him successful. This is how a poor man acquired his own money.

Fortune could come from any means it may be in form of Bank loans, credit cards, charge cards, store cards and you can do something better with all of these things, in as much as whatever you use it for will generate further income, afterwards you can borrow loan for a good course.

CHANNEL EIGHT:

DUBIOUS MEANS

(This is not a recommendation from me but it is still a way of making money.)

This is what I called blood money. Today the young people in our society have turned to this kind of channel to make huge amounts of money, especially teenagers, who like to live in the fast lane, bling life styles. They don't want to follow simple steps or observe any part at science, what they want is a now or never business, due to this fact the majority of youngsters are making money through dubious means, such as selling drugs, guns, illegal materials, internet fraud, stealing or robbery. They take the law into their hands easily and people's lives are nothing to them. Some are even prepared to go to jail and they don't care. Listen to me, this is wrong and it's not a healthy life at all. This is the reason why people are dying at a young age, with a lot of numerous incurable diseases. Silly enough the adults who are supposed to be the role models are also encouraging these young people to commit more crimes.

I personally don't, in any form, encourage dubious means for anyone to acquire money. My main intention is to expose the secret of Satan *"you will know the truth and the truth shall set you free."*

BE CAREFUL HOW YOU MAKE MONEY

You can make your money through fraudulent means [dubious ways], but it is totally not acceptable in the sight of the Lord. Fraud isn't a modern invention; it was around right at the beginning of our generation. ***Gen. 27:30-36***

This was about the story of Jacob supplanting his brother Esau, thereby taking what belonged to his brother in a dubious way, he used it but wasted it at the end of the day. If you are making money through dubious ways, you will surely lose it. There are no two-ways about it. You either lose it now or later, even more than what you acquired originally. Even if you use such money to build a house, surely that property will be sold at a lower price to a righteous person let the unrighteous make their money, they are preparing it for the righteous, because the bible says *"the riches of the gentiles shall be for us."*

Like I mentioned earlier, about the warnings on money obtained through dubious means, the bible says in ***Prov. 13:11*** *"wealth gathered by vanity shall diminish, but he that gather by labor shall increase."* Let what you gather be from your laboring, never you gather from others labor. I see you being successful without dubious means, making your money with ease; I pray there shall never be sorrow attached to your money in Jesus' name.

CHANNEL NINE:

COMPENSATION.

Recently, in the western part of Europe, a new dynamic system has just been introduced which is called no win no fee, people who are wounded as far as several years back, can claim money from where the incident occurred. This is usually done by a group of qualified lawyers who form an association with others to help people claim their rights where there is an accident that is not their fault and many people have acquired a lot of surprise money in this process.

God is a God of re compensation. He knows how to reward people in certain of circumstances. Certain things happen in life and people may have forgotten it so soon, but a time will come when somebody someday will remember and do the right thing. You never know, what incident that you have been involved in the past, might attract compensation in your life.

KNOCK AT YOUR DOOR STEP

I have a close family friend who lived in London for several years, she travelled home one day to visit her mother in their native country and this was during an election campaign. Immediately she settled down after good meal, there was a knock on the door. A group of elderly people walked in to greet my friend's mother and they had brought some good news. A long time ago, the father of my friend's mother's fought for the independence of their town and since the death of the man, nothing particularly had been done for this freedom fighter. The king decided to honor the family by selecting one of the grand-daughters to become a senator who would represent their town's interests in the house of representatives. Of course my friend was nominated in the process to compensate the family. What a story.

Psalm 126. "*When the Lord returned the captivity of Zion, they were like those who dream*"

YOU ARE NOT FORGOTTEN

After the abolition of the slave trade, many families had benefited from compensation which was paid directly to them due to what happened to their relatives. Some grandchildren of past legends, researched their story. Record books were opened and they were remembered and compensation was paid. Not only that, many children received compensation from their parents.

There was another story of a man who managed to buy land in a rural area. After some time, the government detected mineral resources and huge amounts of money were paid and today the man is a multi- millionaire.

YOU ARE DUE FOR COMPENSATION

Like a good house wife who is faithful to her husband, very loyal even when situations were tough, through thick and they would stick to their husband and when the situation turns round the husband may decide to compensate such a wife. Woman you are favored.

Compensation can happen at any level and it can come unannounced. It could be in any form such as insurance, benefits etc. Do you know that God owes some of us?

For some of you who have been dedicated in service, everything you do is from your heart, let me assure you the Lord knows you are due for compensation and surely He shall compensate you in due season.

CHANNEL TEN:

FISH MOUTH (MIRACLE MONEY)

Mathew 17:27 *"Nevertheless, lest we offend them, go to the sea, cast in a hook, and take the fish that comes up first. And when you have opened its mouth, you will find a piece of money take that and give it to them for me and you."*

Do you know that there is still money in mouths of fish? It's called *"miracle money"!* This is the kind of money you don't work for; neither is it gained by fraudulent means. God in his splendor is determined to bless you. He said, 'I will open the floodgates of heaven and will shower you with abundant blessings'.

There was a man who acquired a piece of land covered by garbage.

He had no idea what to do with the piece of land at that particular time, however, the Government requested to buy the land from him (doubling the price he bought it); after investigation revealed that the land was prime for mining the blue diamond and this fact was unknown to him initially.

The man refused to sell, out of great wisdom, knowing full well that for the Government to pay double the price there must be more to it. He approached his solicitor, after the Government threatened to forcefully acquire the land. He was advised to go into partnership with the Government, for a certain percentage of whatever amount of income derived from the minerals generated on the piece of land. The rest is history; there is still miracle money.

Are you aware that the Bank still makes mistakes by accidentally crediting some people's bank accounts? Strange cheques can still be paid by unknown persons directly into your overdrawn account, this is what I call miracle money'.

HERE IS A TRUE LIFE STORY.

A pastor relocated to America from England. The Lord instructed him to start a church over there. He moved into the country, staying in a one room apartment with no furniture. In his dream, the Lord showed him that he was going to bless him with $100,000 someday. Not long after, someone gave him a $10 cheque which he lodged into his account. At a later date, he checked his account balance but to his surprise, found a credit balance of over $100,000 He alerted the bank, he was told by the manager, to his astonishment that the money belonged to him that there wasn't any problem on the account. As he was still arguing with them, he was invited to the Manager's office and to his bewilderment, he was given every dollar in the account and told that the account has been closed, the reason being, they didn't want a trouble maker in the branch. You could see how the Lord's earlier promise came to pass.

I see the Lord doing things that will turn your life around. The bible says 'I will rain my righteousness upon you'. God will rain blessing upon you until there shall be no more room.

In summary, for people to be rich; they may take up a job; establish Business; invest in things that will generate money; discover a fresh talent and make the most of it, put wisdom in place; receive an inheritance; make use of divine inspiration that comes on your way. Others may be fortunate, dubious or whatever, at most you may be compensated. I release unto your hands, the divine blessing of the Lord that makes you rich without sorrow. I decree upon your life, let the blessings of God come upon you and grant you 24 hours miracles in the name of God the Father, the Son, and the Holy Spirit. Let heaven cause it to happen, in Jesus mighty name I pray. Amen.

THE SUMMARY OF THE CHANNELS TO ACQUIRE MONEY

- *GOD DESIRES MANKIND TO OPERATE TO THEIR FULL POTENTIAL ON THIS EARTH AND THIS IS WHY WE ARE FULLY LOADED- PSALM.68:19 .*
- *THERE ARE MANY AVAILABLE CHANNELS TO MAKE MONEY BUT UNFORTUNATELY MANY PEOPLE ONLY CONCENTRATE ON ONE AREA, FORGETTING THAT ACCIDENTS CAN HAPPEN IN LIFE.*

THE FOLLOWING ARE THE CHANNELS TO ACQUIRE YOUR DESIRABLE MONEY

1. WORK OR JOB (EMPLOYEE) – *2 THESS 3:8-11*
2. BUSINESS/INVESTIMENT (EMPLOYER) *MATT. 25:14-18*
3. TALENT/GIFT- *PRO.18:16*
4. WISDOM - *PROVERBS. 4:7-9*
5. DIVINE IDEAS (VISION/DREAM) - *GEN.31:10-12*
6. INHERITANCE **LUKE 15:12** (WILL) *PRO. 13:22*
7. FORTUNES (LOTTERY/GAMBLING/LOANS/CREDIT) **2KINGS.** 4:3-7
8. DUBIOUS MEANS. - **GEN.27:30-35** *PRO. 13:11*
9. COMPENSATION (INSURANCE /BENEFIT)
10. FISH MOUTH (MIRACLE MONEY) - *MATT.17:27*

CHAPTER SIX
THE PRINCIPAL TOOLS NEEDED TO ACQUIRE MONEY

Money frees you from doing things you dislike. Since I dislike doing nearly everything, money is handy. Groucho Marx (1890-1977)

Now that you have identified the channels of money, all you need now are the necessary tools, to acquire your desired money.

Tools are machinery that can help you to carry out your given assignment, ***the better your tools the better the performance***. There are many people with great excellence ideas in our generation but they lack the tools that can help them to do what is necessary and when you know what to do but lack the appropriate tools, it can lead to anger and frustration.

I mentioned earlier that some people have programmed in their mind what they want to be. No matter what book they read or courses they attend, they have determined in their own heart that "**this is how far** *they can go*". But let me warn you, even if you have programmed yourself to the highest level, I encourage you to move to another level of greatness and for you to do this you will need better tools.

EVERYTHING IN LIFE NEEDS THE RIGHT TOOLS

No one on this earth can survive without using tools and each occasion warrants a difference tool. For your information the earth began without form, everywhere was in darkness and before God could do anything, the first tool He used was light which helped to create all things that ever existed on our planet. **Gen.1:1-2** "*In the beginning God created heaven and the earth and the earth was without form and the spirit of God was hovering on water and God said let there be light and there was light*"

Everything you need to do in life requires tools, and you will need some form of equipment to help you to achieve your assignment.

I remember so many times, I was invited to perform in a concert as a gospel artiste, but the system/microphones were not effective (bad). While singing, before I knew it my voice began to crash. I couldn't take the next appointment simply because I had overworked my vocal organ by shouting so loud in order for people to hear what I was singing. We have to look at how we can do to overcome this kind of a problem. I remember one of my friends in the same profession, he contacted the venue beforehand to enquire about the quality of the equipment he had been given. If he found out it was of low quality, he would take along his own equipment to the concert, as it would be unprofessional for people to pay to come and see him sing, only to be disappointed at the standard of performance due to inferior quality of the tools being used. *The better your equipment the better your performance!!!* Some people cook soup, and claim it's not tasty. Why? Because it lacks ingredients. It could simply lacking in something as ordinary as salt.

There are about ten items I classify as principal tools needed to get money. They might be small things, but you need them more than anything else to acquire money.

1. POWER OF IMAGINATION:

When God came to Abraham and said to him, after Lot has departed:

"Look as far as you can see, I will give you as an inheritance" **Gen.13:14**

Imagination is the ability to see beyond. God has given you power to imagine things. Many ideas that come to your spirit enable you to see the big picture. Money is physical and spiritual and you need to imagine it. Don't just sit and wait for it, you must imagine it.

There is power in Imagination; everything in life came into existence due to the power of imagination. The ability to think will lead you to see great opportunities all around you, never leave your mind blank and what so ever you want in life, you need to imagine it before you possess it. What do you see? Some people see failure, some see poverty, weaknesses, trouble and all sorts of unproductive things which are not profitable but rest assured, whatever you see, will determine what you get.

YOU HAVE THE POWER TO PAINT YOUR FUTURE ! YES YOU CAN!

This principle applies to everything, not just to the pursuit of money.

Some people would love to marry but do not have the picture of their desired spouse. Whatever you do not want, never paint that picture in your mind as this will send a wrong signal to the *law of the Universe which says your order is my command*. Most people may not agree with this principle but it's true. What you imagine is what you get.

I remember the story of man who wanted to marry but could not, due to the ignorance of his imagination. As a fine artist he painted a picture of himself alone in the frame and hung the pictures all around his room. One day a friend visited him who noticed the lonely man pictured on the wall and advised his friend to replace the picture of the lone man with that of a couple. At first the picture seemed stupid, but thank God for the spirit of obedience. The fine artist painted another picture of himself with a beautiful woman and started to imagine himself every day according to what he saw in the painting. Three months later the man met a beautiful lady who looked exactly like the woman in the picture and they got married.

Whatsoever you imagine will surely come to reality, most people love certain thing in life such as houses, cars, children, position and many other things but they lack the power of imagination, that's too bad. You must see these things. Let me tell you how powerful imagination is! You can use the power of imagination to undress the most beautiful lady of your choice and see all the nakedness, perform the worst erroneous thing in your heart with such a woman, without anyone to question you. That's how powerful imagination can be. If it is possible for people to imagine wicked things and it came to pass, how much more would it take to imagine the most wonderful thing you wished to have in life. After all, it costs you nothing to imagine and when the fruit is ripe, the benefit are yours.

THE MAGIC POWER OF IMAGINATION

Now if you use the power of imagination on negative things, why can't you use it on positive things? God has prepared something better for you, only people with the right imagination can tap into the future to acquire their need in this competitive world. One thing is still certain, ask the most successful people in life they will all tell you that most things they have today are a result of long time imagination. Keep imagining how wealthy you could be, your dreams, position, your aspiring future. As long as you can imagine, the universe will grant you the right access.

Let me show you the powerful magic of imagination. I called it magic because it's amazing how imagination works. Just take a look at the traffic light, magnificent buildings designed by the architect, the aircraft that flies in the sky, automobiles that drive on the road and a lot of wonderful things that are products of our generation. All these ideas are made possible by the power of imagination. As I am writing this book now someone is imagining certain ideas, either in science, physics, logic, materialism or any professional field. The bible says in the book of **Genesis 11:6** *"And the Lord said, Behold, the people are one, and they are all one language; and this they began to do: and now nothing will be restrained from them, which they have imagined to do.*

Your duty is to imagine whatsoever you need in life and God will make it possible. Money does not grow on the tree but it can be developed in your imagination. How much do you need and how can you get it? This question can be found in the heart of your imagination. So please don't occupy your mind with unprofitable things in life, be positive in your imagination and you will reap the benefits.

PRACTICAL EXERCISE OF IMAGINATION

Now to be practical. I want you to go to a very quiet place where there is no distraction. Close all the doors and switch off your telephone, close your eyes but open your mind and take a tour to the world of the supernatural by imagining a specific thing you need in your life. This could be in any area of your choice, concentrate hard until you are satisfied in your spirit that something has happened. Practice this routine on a daily basis until you see the result according to your imagination. Please don't misunderstand me; this has nothing to do with yoga or other beliefs apart from Christian faith. This will help you to build your faith and whatsoever you stick to, your mind will always manifest and that is the secret.

2: POWER OF POSITIVE CONFESSIONS.

Death and life are in the power of the tongue, and those who love it will beat its fruit. Prov.18: 21

To be Positive means to have the right attitude. Confessions are things that you say out of your mouth for others to witness. Why would a registrar or pastor advise couples, who are in love, to invite friends and relatives to come together and witness them make their marriage vows? Why would they allow you to go through that? It is because, when the confession is made, people will have witnessed it and it becomes an endorsement. They have sealed the confession and by so doing it becomes established.

The law of a country does not come to an existence unless it is pronounced after which it is decreed. That's why the bible says you shall decree a thing first and it shall then be established.

You need to positively confess what you want. I have heard Christians saying they are "broke, that they do not have money" what a sharp arrow of destruction. You need to desist from this kind of pronouncements because they are negative. When the Bible says *"the cattle on the hills are mine, silver and gold are mine, let the weak say I am strong and let the poor say I am rich"*. So where did you get the mind-set of telling people that you are broke? You need to know that whatever you confess is what God will do for you. Some people have rendered their Angels useless because of their idle word; they speak negative things in the presence of their Angels. If you don't mean it; do not say it because your words are like a magnet. Whatsoever you say is what you will attract and according to the law of attraction your wish is their command. Nobody knows who you are until you declare your identity by announcing who you are.

Money is like a spirit, you need to confess positively about it before you can experience the power of acquisition.

MAKE YOUR MONEY REQUEST KNOWN TO GOD

Some people find it difficult to make the request for money known to God in prayer but have no difficulty asking for other requests. What is stopping you from asking for money when you know that money is the answer to all things? There is a power in confession, please begin to confess positively. How can you confess positively? Remember, in the book of Genesis, when God formed the earth, and it was without form, did God beg for light? He said let there be light. And what happened? Light came instantly.

So if God, who created you, could create through words, it proves that words are powerful. When you tell somebody that "I am alive", then yes you are and when you say you are dead, then you better prepare for your funeral. People will accept you the way you prostrate yourself, nobody has an authority over your life apart from you and your words, your confession can build you or tear you down.

BE CAREFUL OF YOUR WORD

I have a spiritual son called John, he was born and brought up in United Kingdom. John suffered from drug and alcohol use, and lived on the streets for over 36 years of his life. He had a number of mental health issues, which God healed miraculously and John was saved completely and he gave his life to Jesus Christ and committed himself to Christian faith.

Out of ignorance, during the terrorist attacks in London, my son John dramatically went to a public phone and dialed the emergency number 999. He told them he had got a bomb and he wanted to blow it up in front of a popular crowded supermarket in town. Of course the police, armed officers with guns, ambulances, and helicopters arrived, stormed the place and arrested John, who later confessed that he was just joking. This action landed John a six month jail sentence with community service, due to what he confessed with his own mouth.

You need to confess positively in any circumstances. God is a positive one that can change negative to positive at all time without seeking permission from anybody. He knows that things could be wrong but He wants you to say it is all right. That's why it is important not to tell people the negative side of what you are going through. If you are sick, tell people that it's well with me, because that's exactly what you want, hence you must confess it. I tell people that sickness will never come to me, because any time I am feeling headache or pain, I do not call it a headache, and I do not call it stomach-pain. That's why in the midst of trouble, I say to myself everything will be all right, you are empowered to make a positive confession. I never confess sickness. Bible also says let the poor say I am rich, God is not teaching you how to lie or be deceitful. Instead, you are being empowered to tap into the Kingdom mentality and in this kingdom, the king does not beg for money. He only needs to speak out and his wishes shall be granted immediately without questioning. Do you know in his kingdom his children are so special, your father owns everything thing including money, the power is in your mouth. Just ask and you might be surprised at the results.

WHAT YOU SAY IS WHAT YOU GET

There is power in positive confession. If you need money, confess it. And when you are confessing, believe it in your heart and it will surely come to pass. You have the power to move mountains from one location to another. All things are possible if you believe and, if put your mind to what you want, it will become to reality.

I remember when I was younger; I said to people around me, that all I needed was just a little money to survive. I wasn't looking for so much money, just enough to get me by. I had been living with that confession for 19 years, until God gave me a vision to start the Christian Club

Houses/Cinema houses, and to establish these; one would need millions of pounds.

When I looked at my account details, I only had in the region of £2000 to £4000 according to my bank account statement. Looking at my financial status the possibility of establishing this vision of cinema houses seemed totally unachievable. One day, I was upset with God, and let this be known while I was praying. God revealed to me about my past negative confession which needed to be renounced.

It was shortly after I changed my narrow-minded confession, that God changed my situation concerning my bank account. I began to experience a supernatural increase of money and now I am functioning well financially, so whatsoever situation you are going through, let positive confession be your priority.

3: THE POWER OF FAITH

Now faith is the substance of things hoped for, the evidence of things not seen. For by it the elders obtained a good testimony. By faith we understand that the worlds we're framed by the word of God, so that the things which are seen were not made of things which are visible. HEBREW 11:1-3

Before you can acquire your desired money, you need to have faith. A faithless man will have nothing to show for his life. Everything in life goes with faith. Faith is your believing system. Unfortunately, many people do not know that they needed faith to acquire money. They have faith in all things but when it comes to money they are faithless.

HOW TO ACQUIRE FAITH

You can acquire faith by hearing, whatsoever you hear determines what you think, and what you think determines what you see and what you see determines what you say. The bible says in the book of **Romans *10:17*** "So then faith comes by hearing, and hearing by the word of God.

The window to your heart is your hearing system, what you hear will determine what you are thinking and what you are thinking will determine what you are seeing, while what you see is what you say and whatever you say will be who you are. If you do not have faith, it will be impossible to achieve your heart desire, faith is in everything that lives on earth.

It is faith that makes you take your medication. You don't know who manufactured the drug but you believe in the doctor who recommended the drug. It is by faith that you go on aircraft, you never know if the pilot is a suicide bomber, but you go on the aircraft because you have faith in the airline according to their records.

Faith is the substance of things hoped for, the evidence of things not seen.

Some of you have given up, thinking that you cannot amount to anything in this nation, but I say unto you that you will amount to something in your life, you will go far beyond your limitations, and God will put the wealth of the nations in your hands. You will arise and you will shine, and achieve greatness because God says so and I believe it.

The *Bible says without faith you cannot please God.*

When a man of God says there is going to be miracle money, some people will doubt the prophecy and other will believe and apply faith. You can hide from people but you cannot hide from God. If I am saying you are going to be rich what is your faith telling you. If your faith says don't mind him, he is just selling his book for money, what kind of work am I doing? Well, you just declared your poverty.

But when you say in your heart that you are going to survive, that God will help me do well and achieve what I want, then the Angels will agree to help you, give you what is needed and they will grant you access to wisdom and every other thing available in the supernatural world that will help to make money making easier to acquire.

Sometimes it may be that you need to sleep on things and then in your sleep ideas come to your mind from all directions after which people are ready to finance your ideas and money will start rolling in.

LET'S KEEP IT REAL

For instance, if someone approaches you telling you that you're supposed to be a hairdresser or maybe you ought to have your own shop. Before you know it you will start thinking about it, weighing the pros & cons, giving it serious thought.

After a while, you start visualizing and seeing shops along the streets with your hairdressing business. You start telling people you are now a hairdresser, business owner or "I am now rich". Where did this idea come from? It came from your hearing system to your thinking system to your seeing system, which invariably then stopped at your speaking system. In other words, what you hear is very important. Have you ever noticed that there are some songs you never like but you keep singing them?

You don't have to see money before you start getting it, as long as you can develop your power of faith, you will surely acquire your desirable money, faith will never disappoint you and you cannot be ashamed if you have faith. The same faith you apply to getting to where you are now is the same you need to acquire money.

FAITH CAN BE A LINK TO YOUR DESIRE

The word of God is very powerful if you believe in your faith and by trusting in the Lord you will get your riches, successes, and prosperity. Do you know that some people who are not Christians do have faith but do not call it faith rather they called it desire? And frankly speaking, their desire will surely move them to another level. To some people it's an intuition; they have an inclination to do something or to act upon an idea which has taken shape in their mind. Christians believe this to be what is called faith, and the power of faith is attached to almost all things in life. Each time you put your faith into action, money will unquestionably to come to you. Faith is like a pregnant woman, who doesn't know the sex of the baby, but she knows something is in her womb even though she can't see it she believes that it's a baby. Everything that is in you, your visions, dreams, and ideas can only be birthed with the power of faith.

4: POWER OF *EXPECTATION.*

This is different from faith or imagination. To expect something means that you are ready and you have it pre-programmed that those things are coming. Just like a goalkeeper in Soccer, when the ball is coming towards his goal-post, he expects that the ball will not pass his standing position into the net. I guess you notice the goal-keeper during penalty taking, he focuses his mind and attention on the ball, and he is ready to catch the ball. You will notice his entire mind, focused on the ball so that it doesn't go past him into the net. So, you must expect things, if you do not expect you will not get, this is how powerful expectation is, *anything you expect becomes your attraction and what so ever you attract you will definitely possess. Acts.3: 1 -6* tells us a story about a lame man at a beautiful gate. The lame man was waiting there, expecting to receive a gift of some sort because he knew that the people who attended the gate of the temple were extraordinary people who could perform miracles and they carry the grace of God.

The man looked at them and expected to receive something from two men called John and Peter, when Peter noticed him he said "Silver and gold I have not, what you are expecting is to be healed. Although people placed you at this gate to beg for money but your expectation is to be able to walk, you want to be whole", and so he was healed. ***The Bible says the expectations of the just shall not be cut off.***

May your expectations never be cut off in the name Jesus Christ.

WHAT ARE YOUR EXPECTATIONS

In this life great things cometh to those who expect things. So what are your expectations? You must be careful of whom you associate with because the expectations of some people stops at the bus-station. Some of your workmates just want to work and die. Is that the kind of dream / vision that you want? This is why you mustn't follow people and mirror their ambitions. Single yourself out and be full of expectations.

Some of you need money but you are not expecting it. Some have a very poor giving and receiving mentality, their attitude is poor, they are not even in the right place. Some do not even know what they want in life, they live in empty world full of lack of expectation, what a stupid mistake to make. Money comes as a matter of expectation, when you develop the mindset of expectation, you will begin to experience money. The amount you want to acquire must be your expectation. The power of expectation will help you to build your mind in a safer mode, the more you develop your ability to expect what you want, the better the attraction will be.

IF YOU WANT MONEY EXPECT MONEY

Everyone have the right to expectation, be truthful to yourself if you need money put your mind to it and have a target. Expectation will allow you to plan ahead and the more you plan and prepare for something the better the reaction. Expectation will also help you to avoid distraction; a good money maker will never waste time in what will disappoint his /her expectation. Do you know that society expects the government to solve some problem and that is why most citizens are disappointed. They expect their parents to lay a money foundation for their future. Instead these people should rely on themselves and put their mind in to achieving something productive, without the reliance of other people.

Always remember nothing in life just happens, you must expect things. If you want money, expect money, programme it into your heart, let it be one of your heart's desires, one day your expectation will surely come to pass and you will enjoy the fruit of your expectations, so what are you waiting for?

5: POWER OF ASSOCIATION

It is the power of influence; your association will determine your life. The people you move with will determine how far you can go. You want to be millionaires, who are your friends? You want to change your job, who are your friends? You want to buy a house, who are your friends? You want to own a mortgage and you still move with friends who live in 1-room council apartments, and they are your advisers. They will never encourage you to go for a mortgage. *Your association will determine how you will acquire your wealth.* How long ago have you approached your friends and ask them for £10,000 to start a new business. Some of you do not know how to control your friends. Everyone who comes to you is just your friend. Do you know that it costs you to have a friend? *Show me your friends and I tell you who you are.*

Some of you have a bad attitude because you have bad people as friends. They have bad attitude towards money. All they do is spend money anyway, without respect. They know all the nooks and corners of West-End, but when it comes to investment they have no idea, they have never invited you to a seminar where you can acquire money or do something to build your future.

ALWAYS STAY CONNECTED

In today's' society, organizations are now starting to join forces. If you want to know, Tesco one of the leading supermarkets in London started as a farmer, but lately they have diversified into other business, such as insurance, credit cart card, electronics, clothing, food stuffs, books, etc. How can a farmer now be involved in these kinds of business activities? It is the power of influence.

If you want to acquire money, the first thing you need to do is build your association, connect yourself with people who know about finance, get closer to those who are where you want to be, build a strong association around them and stick with them until you are able to climb the ladder of finance.

Make an appointment with your banker. Ask if there are any available opportunities in town. Never deceive yourself hoping that any banker will call you from the comfort of their home and give you all the advice in banking. For your information, banks are not allowed to disclose vital information to anybody, except if you contact them before the bird is let out of the cage.

ASSOCIATION IS VERY POWERFUL

Association can also involve you going to your local advice bureau or library to join a financial readers association, who can share information within the group, just make sure you are wise in your collection of associates, if it is not going to be profitable, do not join. Association is very powerful; it will help you to link to your destiny as quickly as possible. After all, little drop of water becomes a mighty ocean, association will grant you access to information and information is money. If you move with a group of poor people, the tendency is there for you to be poor, and with a group of the rich people you will surely be rich. So the people you move with will determine your future.

6. POWER OF APPRECIATION.

When God does something for people, they don't know where the power comes from, they attribute everything to themselves. They say to themselves, *"I have tried, among seven siblings in the same family, am the richest. I have tried."* And so on and so forth. The money you refused to appreciate will surely depreciate. You see a millionaire and you despise him. You despise people with new cars saying they all live on fraud! You need to appreciate wealthy people. It is a secret of life. Even God loves it.

Psalm.150 "Let everything that has breath praise the Lord."

Whatsoever you appreciate will be what comes to you. Appreciation does not just limited to saying thank you alone. It depends on what you are thinking towards successful people. When you see someone progressing, say to yourself, "Thank God". If it is possible, make them your Mentor, don't despise them.

There are many things in life you can appreciate, such as money. If the Bible says money answers everything, you need to appreciate money and the power of money every time you come across any amount, be it a little or large amount.

My mother gave me some good counsel when I was growing up. She said "If anybody gives you a penny when you're expecting a thousand, never despise such a giver. The person may disappoint you today or may even be testing your relationship. If you can get rid of bitterness and still go forward to express your gratitude for that little amount, the giver, due to your appreciation, will be encouraged to give you a bigger amount in the future".

A LITTLE EFFORT MAKES A GREAT DEAL

I heard a story of a pastor who publicly disgraced a man for donating coins inside the church basket offering. The man was highly disappointed and walked away from the church. Not quite long after, the Lord blessed the same man with great riches and one day the same man of God went to another church for a building fund raising event. There the man was called out for a donation and he blessed the church with £4,000,000. This is the power of appreciation at work; had the brother who gave the smaller amount been appreciated, by now the pastor would have been the one who will be enjoying the wealth of the man.

APPRECIATION IS A SECRET OF WEALTH

Everybody loves to be appreciated, no matter how little; giving thanks is part of everyday life. It is a secret weapon and whoever knows the secret will enjoy the fruit thereafter, *great people live their lives daily on appreciations*, *what you appreciate will never, ever be abuse*. Any student who appreciates the efforts of their teacher will be a brilliant student. The worker who appreciates the position of their employer will soon be promoted, if you can appreciate life you will live successfully.

Appreciation goes beyond just a word, sometimes you can buy a little gift and present it to people in your life, you can make just a phone call to people who make things happen in your life, extending goodness to others in your surroundings, you then can return back to the place of your humble beginnings and reward them. You can send flowers, post cards, money, and even just talking about them in a positive way. All these are what I call appreciation and whenever you do all of these things, you can make your life successful. Do you know that people love to be closer to people who appreciate things? Life is not about just grumbling and complaining, when your heart is full of appreciation you can see clearly all the opportunities around you and *the opportunities you make use of will determine the money you will acquire*.

Some people look straight to their mother and despise them by saying to them, "You, poor woman. What did you give to me apart from life?" Do you know that life is worth more than money? If the mother had aborted such children years ago they would never have existed. Learn to be appreciative and you will see money coming to you.

7. POWER OF ACTION

*Then **Caleb** quieted the people before Moses, and said, "Let us go up at once and take possession, for we are well able to overcome it." (Numbers13:30)*

This is the movement of reality taking the steps when you hear the sound of the rain which you have been expecting, most people have the greatest faith that can move mountains; they have a very strong association with faith, being very well connected but they lack action. Some are good in planning, great thinkers with excellent skills, having the whole world in their hands but the only thing they lack is the ability to take action. You've wanted to go to the University for the past 7 years, you've wanted to better your life by changing your job for the past 20 years and you want to leave your council flat but you're still there after 17 years with no action. You have been saying you want to buy your house for how many years now?

ACTION IS LOUDER THAN VOICES

People are only recognized in life for the actions they have taken. Nobody recognizes mediocrity. The action you implement will determine your name in the Guinness book of records. Some of you are better than others who are out there. There are good musicians, good hairdressers, but how long ago have you been planning to set up your business? Meanwhile, those who are not as good as you have started theirs, and using you as their adviser.

You must take action. There are "action-people" on Earth; all they need is someone giving the instructions. As you are reading this script about finances, some of you are ready to take action, while others are ready to read it a million times, looking for the mistakes in it. At the end of the day, there are some who will quickly acknowledge the authenticity and the points in this book and will immediately go into action, making use of all the enumerated points and be on the path of making their money.

The time you waste cannot be regained and the earlier you take action, the better you achieve your dream. Some people are hoping for tomorrow, forgetting that today is what you have. No man owns tomorrow. ***It's best to show ones' actions, than a hundred sheets of planning.*** Please don't get me wrong. It is very good to plan, but a plan without action equals to no plan at all. Actions are louder than voices, all the planning in your heart demands action. A life without action is no life, just like a pregnant woman who is happy to carry a baby in her womb for a good nine months and when the time of delivery comes, she is afraid to push. This is how bad it is when you have great ideas without action.

A TEXT MESSAGE THAT PROVOKED ACTION

I remember, one day as I was taking my shower the Lord spoke to my spirit that I should send a text message to all the people in my phone contacts, which I fully obeyed. The message was "*what is it that the Lord is saying to you right now about the plans in your heart. Please don't waste time, take action now and go for it.*" These messages challenged a lot of people who took my message personally and a lot of people shared their testimonies with me and today many people are fulfilling their visions, thank God for the obedience of taking action in sending the text and for the people who were challenged with the message in the text and then into taking action. Do you know that while others took action, some still procrastinated and as such, these people still remain where they are.

JUST STEP OUT

You too can take action now. Forget about all the excuses. Successful people overlook obstacles; they overcome their fear by taking the necessary action. If others can take action, you can do the same, open your eyes wide. Money is everywhere, the action you take will determine how much you get, stand up, go out, look for positive action to take immediately, you have being planning for such a long time. There are many visions that God has already laid into your heart. What you need now is the action that must be taken, go for it and God will see you through in Jesus' name.

8. THE POWER OF POSITIONING

It is the ability to be in the right place, at the right time, doing the right thing, for the right purpose, that produces the right results.

Some people are out of position, just like an amoeba that has no shape. They blend into anything that requires an easy decision without thinking of the outcome, only thereafter to face regret and shame. If you offer such people an early-morning cleaning job, they are there. Offer them a late night job, "key job", they are interested. Some study very hard at their schools and obtain great excellent results, some spend many years achieving a degree but unfortunately only end up in accepting anything that comes their way without remembering what they have studied in school. How long do you want to be a servant when God is calling you to be a master? How will you feel when all the traffic lights on the road are not functioning? How will you feel when you wake up and the light refuses to shine? How will you feel if the air ceases to be?

EVERYTHING IN LIFE NEEDS POSITIONING

All these things are placed in position by God and men. You need to arrange your life. Only those who position themselves will receive the benefits of what they are working for.

You should always ask yourself this question; why are some people having a better life while others are still living in absolute degrading poverty? I mentioned earlier that the gap between the rich and the poor is wisdom and your wisdom starts from your positioning.

I do not mean to write against what you are doing but to check, re-examine what you have been doing and put things in a rightful order. Everything in life needs to be positioned and you can do it as long as you are willing. Your sorrow and pain will soon be over especially if you are single lady reading this book; the Lord will give you the man of your desire. But if you desire a better man, you need to position yourself, stop fooling around with a man who is a time waster. Focus on your future; you deserve the best in life.

POSITIONING WILL OPEN THE RIGHT DOOR

What I do mean by positioning yourself? For instance, if you want to be a millionaire don't move around with a thousand minded people who are going just there. They will cause accidents along your way. All they are talking about is what they know. Go and befriend millionaires, buy them gifts. If you need a car, position yourself with a car owner; that's called positioning.

There was one of my ministers in the church who loved God with all his life and who was very dedicated. One day he collected my car, drove it to a petrol station, filled the tank and also washed the car. I happened to buy another car shortly so I decided to sell my old car. Meanwhile the Minster that filled my tank and washed my car was looking to buy a car, when I discussed this with my wife we both agreed to bless the man with our old car. That is how the man became the owner of the car. The most interesting part is that the car tank was still filled with the petrol and sparkling clean. Whatsoever you need make sure that you are positioning yourself.

9. THE POWER OF RIGHTEOUSNESS.

The righteous shall flourish like a palm tree; He shall grow like a cedar In Lebanon. those who are planted in the house of the LORD shall flourish in the courts of our God. They shall still bear fruit in old age; they shall be fresh and flourishing. **PSALM 92:12-14**

What does it take to be righteous? **LIVING RIGHT**. It's as simple as ABC. When I became a believer, the word righteous was a big theological concept to me. I thought that to be righteous meant you must observe some religious rituals, flying to heaven, be connected to some popular angel and above all, separate yourself away from people and that you must be deep in your faith. Righteousness is not only limited to someone who believes in God, going to church or any other place of worship and believe in heaven. Rather it means *anybody who wants to be successful and have a good relationship should learn to live right and living right is an act of righteousness.*

The Bible says.....*Tell a righteous man that it shall be well with him, because he will reap the fruit of his labor. A righteous man shall flourish like a palm tree.*

You can also acquire money when you live right. Some people don't know how to live right; they spend their money on rubbish stuff, going to places where they are not supposed to go and doing all sorts of abominable things.

Researchers have proven that if you are over 25years of age, there is a tendency that over a million pounds must have passed through your hands since you were born. However, because some of us have not been living right this money vanishes via unnecessary spending, going to pub/clubhouses, attending/organizing parties.

A righteous man will flourish like a palm tree, which means, when you are righteous everything about your life is productive. The brain in your head will develop great ideas; the word of your mouth will produce wisdom, your name on any label will carry power. In fact everyone will want to deal with you and when this happens tell me how will you not acquire as much money as you like in life? But who will want to associate with someone who is not living according to the right expectations in life? No matter what happens to a man who lives right, everybody will rise up for the help of a righteous man. The Bible says *a righteous man may fall 7 times, he will surely rise again.*

If you are living right, your whole being is full of positive thinking. You never live in fear because you are bold like a lion, nothing will move you.

You can face anybody and be connected to anybody in society, both the poor and the rich will find you interesting, governments will be ready to grant you any assistance, even foreigners will interact with you on business matters. Everybody wants to be a friend to those who are righteous. Do you ever trust people who are not righteous with your money? No.

If a drug addict person comes to you for £10,000 to start a business will you give him the money? Some of you live that way. You need to live right, walk right, study the right books, and listen to the right and useful sermons. I remember the story of a lady that was brainwashed by a so called prophet and she believed that her mother was the main cause of her not being prosperous. She eventually used petrol to douse her mother and burnt her alive, not knowing that it was because she didn't position herself in the right place, that was causing her to be unsuccessful. The lady in question was later jailed for her wrong action.

If you need to acquire money you should start living right and stop blaming your incapacity on other people. The bible says there is a future for a man that lives right.

10. THE POWER OF SEED.

A rich man knows what to do for society before he makes money. What does he do? He makes sure that he supports every charity project around the town. So when any position or contract props up, it's the rich that will come to mind first before any other person, because of the good he has done for society. (I.e. the seed he sews in the past). You need to sow seeds of good in others to acquire money. I am not talking about someone asking people to contribute to a course. I'm talking about knowing exactly what you have to do just going ahead and doing it. Your tithe is an example of the kind of seed I am talking about. You need to pay your tithe before things become tight for you. You need to be faithful with your tithe. A good farmer will never eat a seed, no matter what, but some people eat their seed. Everything that comes into their hand goes to their mouth; this is why many people don't have enough reserve.

Many people in our society have no regard for the principles of life, one of which is that your first income/salary is supposed to go to your parents who labor over you. If you have spent your first salary without giving to your parents, you have then sown the seed of poverty. I say unto you now, if you want to be rich, calculate how much and pay same to your parents and tell them this is the money I should have given to you long time ago {being my first salary}. The moment you do that you will witness the heavens opening for you miraculously. You may say but we do not practice this in our culture, I am not writing about a cultural system here, this is a principle and principles work everywhere. The bible say honor your parents for all your long days and that you should give your first salary to your parent. You should honor them with your fruit of labor.

The prayer they will offer on your behalf will open heaven for your sake and many blessing will come upon your finance for the rest of your life.

Seed is so important that a farmer, he who eats his seed will surely harvest nothing. Put your seed to where it belongs, because with it you can acquire your desirable money. May the Lord bless you.

It is the will of God for you to prosper, and the more you recognize God the more successful you will become. *3John 2* says *Beloved, I pray that you may prosper in all things and be in health, just as your soul prospers. The more you remember God the more you prosper.*

When you honor God with your seed He will honor you with his blessing,

ECCL 11:1 says "Cast your bread upon the waters, for you will find it after many days. *The seed you refuse to sow will be the harvest you will never have.*

SUMMARY OF THE PRINCIPAL TOOLS NEEDED TO ACQUIRE MONEY

1. IMAGINATION: *EVERYTHING IN LIFE CAME TO EXISTENCE DUE TO POWER OF IMAGINATION- **GEN. 13:14.***
2. POSITIVE CONFESSION - ***PRO.18:21.***
   WHAT YOU HEAR - DETERMINES WHAT YOU THINK - WHAT YOU SEE – WHAT YOU SAY.
3. FAITH (DESIRE) ***HEBREW 11:1-6.***
4. EXPECTATION. - ***ACTS 3:1-6*** *(GREAT THINGS CAN ONLY HAPPEN TO THOSE WHO HAVE EXPECTIONS)*
5. ASSOCIATION. (POWER OF INFLUENCE)- ***PSALM 133.*** *THE PEOPLE YOU MOVE WITH WILL DETERMINE YOUR FUTURE.*
6. APPRECIATION. ***2 SAM .6:12-19*** *(WHAT YOU DO NOT APPRECIATE WILL DEPRECIATE)*
7. ACTION. ***NUMBERS.13:30*** *(YOU ARE ONLY RECOGNISED FOR THE ACTION YOU TAKE)*
8. POSITIONING.- ***2 KINGS 1:1-15*** *(DOING THE RIGHT THING IN THE RIGHT PLACE AT THE RIGHT TIME)*
9. RIGHTEOUSNESS. - ***PSALM 92:12-14*** *(LIVING RIGHT IS LIVING HEALTHY IN LIFE)*
10. THE POWER OF SEED. ***MARK 4:1-9*** *(A GOOD FARMER WILL NEVER EAT A SEED NO MATTER WHAT)*

CHAPTER SEVEN
PROVOCATION OF MONEY

Money is like a sixth sense without which you cannot make a complete use of the other five. W. Somerset Maugham

I mentioned earlier that the desire to acquire money is **far beyond imagination but rather provocation,** without smoke, there is no fire. The Lord is about to take you to another level, and you must not take it lightly. I see God taking you into another level, in Jesus' name. Amen. No matter what it takes, your God will make it happen.

In the previous chapter, I enumerated the basic tools needed to be acquired; it will be totally impracticable to use those tools without considering certain aspect. How many of you know that life is not as easy as it seems on the surface, but something always leads to something.

Having a dream of money is not enough but when you wake up into monies reality, that's when you become aware of what is going on around you. Some of you go to sleep at night, shattered and broke when you go to bed, but whilst asleep, pictures appear in your mind of being a millionaire. Whilst in your dream, you were proclaimed to be so, only to wake up in the morning and still find yourself in abject poverty. Such things are so severe in our lives.

It's one thing to dream and another thing to wake up to reality. Practical application accounts for everything. What you do practically is what people see in you. All those years of experience at your place of work or profession is your own making, what really matters most is your achievement.

LACK OF MONEY RAISES MANY QUESTIONS

Remember the word of God says "Money answers all things", the problem is when there is lack of money, it means there will be many questions. For instance, the house you live in, you know for sure that you have stayed there for so long and you need to move to a better place, the

salary being paid to you at work is something you dislike, and you are not happy with the work you do. All these can lead to unnecessary provocation if there is no money in the pocket. Although there is nothing wrong in being angry because it makes you take the necessary steps and move to the next level, especially positive and good anger.

THE BETTER SIDE OF ANGER

Life is full of many provocations and anything can make you get angry. To be angry is not the problem but the outcome of anger means a lot, whatsoever you see here on the surface of the earth is as a result of somebody anger who believes in a change, not comfortable with their environment tab and they wish to do something special to prove there is a better way out, Meanwhile, it going to be shameful for getting angry with others without taking the necessary step. No matter what anybody says about your situation do not just get angry but do something.

Remember, someone calling you a poverty-stricken old fool about three years ago, and the next two years, you are still on the same level of poverty without any single improvement; then something is wrong with you. When people or situations get you angry, you need to step out to a better life. There is nothing wrong with anger; it helps especially when it is a good anger.

When someone refers to you as a single parent and all you do is get angry even to the extent of letting that anger affect your children, that's not the kind of anger I am talking about, that comment is invariably challenging your God, and should make you angry with yourself thereby asking yourself some salient questions as in: why am I still unmarried? Could it be my dressing? Could it be my attitude towards men that is making me to still remain unmarried? Try to take a step towards changing that situation so that next you are seen with your husband, the people who made the initial comments will now be in jealous mood, because your level has changed. When you are provoked, the next reasonable thing is to change the cause of action; you can walk away and do the right thing.

There are things that provoke people to acquire money. You don't just pluck the fruit from on top of the tree somebody has to plant the tree before the fruits come. There is story behind every success, anyone you see that is successful, that success didn't just come ordinarily.

Among many things that can provoke people to set up a goal and start the raise of success are the following:

1. THE ANGER OF POVERTY.

What is poverty? By my own interpretation, poverty is a disease which can be linked to a curse. According to the dictionary poverty means someone else taking credit for the hard-work you are doing.

The fear of poverty has caused more pain than the victory out of poverty. Most people are afraid to be poor yet they are still poor. I remember before the writing of this book, I preached this message to our congregation(ICCC NORTH LONDON) as a result of the Holy Spirit's direction. It happened that many people in the church are complaining of a lack of money and the Lord instructed me to teach the body of Christ on the subject of how to acquire money, immediately I got the messages ready for the audio CD available for sales, to my surprise out of all the topics about 10 series the most sold out was the topic of poverty and that was when the Lord opened my eyes of understanding to know that people are afraid of poverty but there was not much action on how to overcome it.

Nobody loves to be poor, most times circumstances may warrant it and result to anger. This anger should provoke you to take a new step into the place of you fulfilling your destiny.

I came from a rich home as a very successful man. When my father died, all he had then went down after his demise because he didn't apply the principles of wisdom. In view of this, I was brought up by my mum in hardship. She had to send us to different places {family relatives}, but I was fortunate enough to be the only one that stayed with her then. She had desired to send me to one of the best schools, but couldn't afford the money.

Thanks be to God that I was able to fend for myself and went to school to learn English Language, without which I would have been relying on an interpreter to communicate with you. So this is why I said Poverty is a Curse.

At this juncture, I implore you to go through these passages in the Bible: Psalm *66:12* says: ***You have caused men to ride over our heads; we went through fire and through water; but you brought us out to rich fulfillment.***

Why is it that today somebody decides how much you pay for the room you live in?

Some people live in a Council Flat, and are comfortable living there, simply because they pay a little amount of money, however, the day the Council decides to evict them, that is the day it will dawn on them that things have changed. And because they didn't make adequate preparations for such an incident, that's when they will find out what it means "for someone to ride over their head".

Most people cannot decide when to go, how to go, where to go as a result of limitation. {However I see your story changing in Jesus' name Amen}. Every limitation in your life will be removed and God will free you from the power of oppression.

You may have been going through some difficulties and trials, but God is not stopping your life. Your life is not at a full stop, no, you are passing through. It is a challenge for you to move to another level. When you are poor, and cannot afford what other people can afford, it is a big pain, such pain should not die like that; rather it should help to prompt you to move to another level.

The Rich in the society are becoming richer while will you want to be content with being poor, poverty is a bad mentality and it's not in God's dictionary. God said *"In the land you are going to possess, poor people will not cease to exist, but don't let it be, God is saying "Settle them."* How can you settle the poor while you are also poor? Poverty is a provocation that is supposed to move people to another level.

No matter how poor you may be just let it move you into the place of riches. You must not allow poverty to pull you down. Although it may be a curse, but thank God, the Bible says "No man can curse whom God had blessed". You need no running around to seek for help; God is your help in time of trouble. He is the only One that can help in changing your situation. Little do you know that you are serving the God of Miracle, who can supply all your riches. *Philippians 4:19 "And my God shall supply all your need according to His riches in glory by Christ Jesus".* So let that poverty provoke you with a view to acquiring your desirable wealth, and you will get there in Jesus' name. Amen!

2. FAILURE

It is the ability of not been able to meet up with expectations. You are not poor but you failed because you cannot meet up. To fail means after giving all your effort, time or energy things couldn't work out as expected. When someone fails the heat that develops in such a heart is very precarious. Failure most time will make some people also develop hatred on those who are successful which is not supposed to be, but rather, the anger of Failure should provoke you to a point that you tell yourself, my father failed, my mother failed, but I am not going to fail. In the past I have failed, but from now on *no more failure*.

At any point in time, failure in any field of life should not become a negative influence to the extent of driving your life to the pit, instead failure should be taken as a stepping stone to provoke you to a place of wealth after all nobody wishes to be a failure in life.

TURN FAILURE TO YOUR SUCCESS

There was this story about an American, who graduated from the University and couldn't get employment anywhere he went. Along the line, he will go out of his apartment and pick newspapers to read invariably and bring it home, just to keep himself busy. All the while, the whole room became filled up with newspaper; he now brought out his bed and made use of the paper pack as a bed and table and the likes. It got to a stage that all his friends and relatives branded him as "Paper-man" to the extent that they would call him to come and pack all available papers in their places.

He said to himself, he doesn't want to be a failure, hoping that all will be well. One day, while on his normal daily walk, he saw an advertisement by a company requesting for used papers which they re-cycle for their products. He went there to enquire, at the end of the day, the company came for the papers he had collected {mind you, it was a lot} and before you know it, he was paid $1million for the whole thing. This was how an "ordinary Paper-man" became a Millionaire.

You will notice from this story that failure itself is not something that will make you to give-up but should provoke/propel you to taking decisions that will move you to another level.

No matter how many times you fail, you've got to keep trying till success comes your way. When you fail, there is still success lying ahead. The only people that fail and die are those who have never tried anything. The inventor of the Electric bulb, Thomas Edison, tried so many times {over 5oo times} before he got it perfected, but today his failure has turned to success. I see your failure turning to success. **(Read Judge 6: 1-14)**

JUST TRY A LITTLE BIT MORE

Never give up on yourself no matter how many times you fail, keep on trying and encourage yourself. Winners never quit only quitters never win. People around you may call you a failure but see beyond their limitations. Nobody can put a stop to your life except yourself, I know it is very painful after putting in all your efforts only to discover that you've been unsuccessful, you feel like no strength remains or like life is treating you unfairly. Stop blaming your failure on people it's time to renew your mind, put on a new attitude or better still change the style of your performance, do something new if you want a better result. Most people you see today who are successful, they are the product of yesterday's failure who never gave up, if you want to acquire money you must learn how to deal with failure because money never comes easily especially if you need much.

3. CHALLENGES

There are many challenges in life; it is another provocation that can help you to acquire money. These are the difficult things you are going through in your life. Just like in the Bible there was a story of a man called Jabez. *1Chron.4: 9-10*.

"Now Jabez was more honorable than his brothers, and his mother called his name Jabez, saying, "Because I bore him in pain." 10 And Jabez called on the God of Israel saying, "Oh that you would bless me indeed, and enlarge my territory, that your hand would be with me, and that you would keep me from evil, that I may not cause pain!" So God granted him what he requested.

The name Jabez means son of sorrow because the mother gave birth to him during labor pain. Instead of him allowing that sorrow to weigh him down, he used that sorrow to plead to God for a change of name. And God blessed him and he was more honorable more than his brothers. Today his story is in the Bible.

No matter the challenges you can set a goal from any present situation in life. What you are faced with now, you can set it as a goal to acquire your money, challenges can be in any category, families, healthy, status, accommodation etc.

There was man called Oyenusi in Nigeria. In those days, he was going through various challenges in life, one day He was visiting his friend during a raining season and was walking along the road, putting on white lace. On his way, a driver splashed dirt on his white cloth and to make matters worse, he was insulted by this driver. The aftermath of that encounter made him to become so angry {remember—poverty} that he swore to himself that he was going to have money no matter the circumstances, however, he chose a bad path {armed robbery} in fulfilling that vow.

There may be challenges you are faced with, those challenges are not to make you bow your head in failure but to make you take decision for a better tomorrow. Life is all about choices, if you choose the right choice you will benefit rightly and if you decided on the wrong side you will also leave with it throughout your life time.

YOU CAN CHALLENGE YOUR CHALLENGES

Also, I have a solicitor friend who many years ago was arrested and locked in a detention camp for him to be deported back to his native-land. He was camp picked up on the day he was ordained an Elder in the Church. While in detention, he was so angry that after working so hard in the country why it must be him that is meant for deportation. Right there, he made a vow that he was going to be a solicitor when he is released and bail out people in this kind of situation, to the Glory of God; he is a Solicitor bailing people in immigration problem.

I see God moving you in the area of your challenges. *Challenges will come but let it prepare you for next level*. There may be many things you are faced with now, never see it as obstacles instead use it as opportunity to acquire money. However some of you just feel so guilty and bury your head in shame/failure and weeks after weeks you attend church service with a view to collecting another medication, I renounce that spirit from you, no condition is permanent you can challenge your challenges. The situation you are in, is not a condemnation, God put you in that situation for the benefit of your future.

NOT AS DIFFICULT AS YOU THINK

I remember how I became a video producer, the true story started back in late 80s when I was launching my musical group, it was my first big day in my musical career, people of highly caliber were invited and the event took place in one of the most sought after venue,. Before the event a videographer was introduced to me who claimed to work with the national television authority, a substantial of money was paid and on the day of celebration the man came with big video equipment, lighting everywhere, in fact it was so good that I was confident that when the video is produced I will be able to market the production successfully. To my surprise when the video got to me I was highly disappointed to the extent I could not watch the video for a second time due to the poor production. With this challenge I promised to study about video production and today I am a qualified videographer with the passion to train people all around me. I know you've also got your own story wrapped round your subsist, you can turn the ladder around. It's not as difficult as you think, it may be a second chance, you can still take a new step or any which way, do something and you will be amazed by the result of your decision.

CHALLENGING CONDITION IS NO EXCUSE

Some people are single parents; they bow down their head into singleness, instead of thinking about what they can do. Do you know they can become a counselor for every single lady in the community and establish a therapy counseling them at a cost.

May be you are unemployed for so many years, you can write a book through that, and tag it as "My Life as an Unemployed". Take it to Job Centre; you will see people buying it.

Every challenge in your life is to take you to another level. Go with your current challenges and fulfill your dreams. If what you are doing doesn't work, change it. Don't bury your head in your hand and complain to God that things are difficult, stop using your condition as an excuse. You were born to win, if while you are in your mother womb you've fought the challenges of life and you came out a winner, how much now that you are surrounded by many helpers of destiny who can assist you to fulfill your goals. So don't let your present challenges bury your head in your hand but to propel you unto the next level.

4. OPPORTUNITY

Opportunities abound everywhere. And in everything there is always opportunity. Whatsoever you are going through, there are always opportunities which you can use to acquire money. You should always learn to take advantage of things. Do you know that chances come to people at times and they let go without making use of them. Opportunity comes every day of one's life, everything around us is an opportunity but when we fail to use it, that's when we become a failure. You can use opportunity as a means of challenges, removing yourself from failure, and taking yourself out of poverty. ***Opportunity is something that comes your way like chances***. Don't misuse your chances.

THE DOWNFALL OF MAN IS NOT
THE END OF HIS LIFE

There was this story of an African man based in Germany for over 15 years without proper legal resident permit. He was apprehended by the Immigration officers, and later deported. While in the plane on his journey back home, he met a business man who promised to help him by sending him back to Germany to be his company's representative with a mouth-watering remuneration.

As God would have it, he got back into Germany working for the businessman. He was entrusted with the finances of the business transactions. Along the line, a huge sum of money was remitted to him in Germany for procurement of drugs for the company in Africa. At this time, there was delay in the production of the consignment and the money so remitted had to be kept with him for about 2 months. He quickly thought of this as an opportunity to make use of the money, the man eventually came up with a plan by buying trailer vehicle with container back, loaded with motto spare parts, shipped it to Nigeria and made so much money out of it. After some time, the businessman had to tell him that his services won't be needed any longer because his own brother is coming to take over the business. Without agitation, he told the business man what he did with the money while it was in his custody. What a great opportunity.

This is the kind of opportunity/chance I was talking about. Make use of your opportunity to acquire your desirable wealth. Opportunity comes in different forms, sometimes it may come unannounced depending on what side it takes, contrary to what people believe, opportunities come every time. You only have to see it and the more you make use of it, the better the chances of making money.

OPPORTUNITY IS IN EVERYTHING

Sometime ago I had a discussion with a young lady who newly gave birth to a beautiful baby girl. At the time of giving birth, the government refused to give her and the baby support due to some circumstances, she was so bitter about the situation and I decided to counsel her, the lad in question was a very wonderful, caring, loving and well-spoken of by people, she can do anything to satisfy any one that come on her way. Immediately she came to me, she was lamenting on lack of money and the fear of how can she look after the newly born baby, she also said she was desperately in need of £100 (hundred pounds) to meet with an urgent matter, I asked her one question "how do you think you can raise this money" she busted into cry out of confusion. I finally calm her down and asked another question "Do you have ten people among your friends who have not seen your child since you have given birth?" She told me that she got more than ten friends but what can that do to her financial needs? She questioned frankly.

I advised her to pay a surprise visit to all the ten top loving friends around her with the newly born baby and as you may know, the lady is of African origin and the culture demands that when you are visited by a newly born baby, they come with good luck and the best way to activate this blessing is by giving money and of course everybody will love to give generously to a visiting baby mother most especially the little baby who is very beautiful. This was how a newly baby became an opportunity instead of liability.

TURN YOUR MESS INTO YOUR MESSAGE

Your culture may not warrant the above story but opportunity can arrive in any condition you find yourself, I have also counsel a single mother instead of staying idle and complains of lack of money, she can as well inform some friend, neighbors' or relative to use the opportunity of looking after another baby and in return money will come, far still if you are going through certain mess, you can share your experience either through seminar or book and your mess will become your message.

The most successful people in our planet do not just arrive in the present situation you see them now. These people make use of opportunity and the more opportunities you make use of, the better chances of money you can acquire.

Look out for what so ever the worse situation around you, create an opportunity out of it and you will be glad that money will come, remember money is everywhere and money is in everything. You can only have money if you can see it.

5. HISTORY/BACKGROUND

Now Jephthah the Gileadite was a mighty man of valor, but he was the son of a harlot; and Gilead begot Jephthah. Judge 11:1

The man Jephthah who was born out of wedlock, he was a cast-away from his people and being born as a son of harlot, he cannot be allowed to do anything in the society, in the actual fact this man's life supposed to be a failure. However, he didn't allow his background to move him to a negative path. He later left the family and move to the bush to learn war tactics. When the time for war came, the people called on him and he made use of the situation at hand by bargaining for a position of leader which was agreed; today his name was registered in the history of Israel as the leader of leaders.

You may not be able to change your background or ancient times, but you can change your environment, your character and change your habits. Your history or background should not make you act like a lunatic.

Every nation got their own history or background which people can actually identify with in any which way- either good or bad. For example, it has been registered that Jamaicans are drug addicts. You don't have to come abroad and use that history to destroy your lives; instead you should use that fact to make a positive impact on the society.

Likewise, Nigerians are tagged fraudsters, do they have to travel abroad and be duping people? Your background is supposed to make a positive impact in your life and provoke you to be a better person.

Some people's family history may contain failure, rather than allowing that to set them back it should be the way forward.

Champions never set back because of their past, instead the past is what motivate them into a better future. You may not have been born with a golden spoon in your mouth; it's your duty to ensure a golden spoon in your own children's mouth. A failure person will always have many excuses, blaming people for their malfunction.

Although life may seem unfair to some people, but it's your right to play fairly with life by producing the best for the future and to leave an inheritance for your next generation.

EAGLES ARE BORN TO FLY

Thomas Edison the inventor of electric bulb which left our planet with many lighting today was surrounded by the earth full of darkness with only sun and moon acting as the most fascinating object of the day. Your history may look as if no one in your family who ever emerge as a rich man, you can create a history of success through the power of your imagination and make use of your creativities God has dropped in your mind, the more you renew your mind from the nightmares of the past, the brighter the future.

You have the power to turn your family failure into the ocean of wealth, nothing just happened, you can make it happen through the anger of your family background or any history that may have been recorded in your history, remember the eagles are born to fly higher, you can make the money of your choices.

Kindly let your background provoke you unto the level of acquiring your wealth. President Obama of United State of America has played his own part. See yourself as been greater than Obama. Don't let people abuse you of your color and label you as useless entities. Look at yourself as one of the richest man on Earth. Make that story and let it be your portion.

6. STUDY OR EDUCATION

"Study and be eager and do your utmost to present yourself to God approved (tested by trial), a workman who has no cause to be ashamed, correctly analyzing and accurately dividing [rightly handling and skillfully teaching] the Word of Truth". 2Timothy2:15

lack of knowledge has taken over our generation over the years, especially the young adult even despite their many years of learning in the school still they are illiterates, you will find out some people with great certificates and qualifications yet they are unemployed. The more you study the better you should know and what you know is what you possess, to study may be the ability to learn new skills, ability to use wisdom.

Due to studies a lot of people have discovered many great assets to acquire money of their choices. The more you read the story of successful people the better you understand the miseries that surround their success. For your information money has a language and the more you learn money language the better you will acquire money. There are inspirational books written by great people that can provoke you, the more you read the better you perform. If you really want to be successful in this competitive world, you need to be well enlightened; money lies in the power of information and information come from intensive study.

TREASURES ARE HIDDING INSIDE A BOOK

As the adage goes nothing new under the heaven, whatsoever you want to be in life somebody used to be and their experience can be found in the books, all the greatest people that ever leave are great readers, readers are leaders, if you are ready for change, you need to study your family history, get to know why situation where not favorable in their life and see how you can address the situation differently after all better days are ahead of you.

The more you study situation the better you can provide the solution. Study will provoke you to find solution, ignorance is a disease and excuse is not the answer either, the power to your desirable wealth is in education, if you are tired of failure, read successful books or if you need to improve your physical health condition read healthy book, no matter what you wish to know, spiritual, politics, families etc. Help yourself go out to the bookshop and buy the books of your choices, attend lectures, seminars and so forth.

Study to be well approved and break the barrier of ignorance, good treasures are hiding inside the book, all you have to do is to find all the relevant subject that can move your life forward, although useful information may cost you money and demand your time or intention, what worth doing worth doing it best, search for the truth, sell what you have if possible to acquire the knowledge you needed for your success, never let anything stand on your way of study, create a better life and glorious future by study all the available information at your reach then you can possess the power to acquire money or the better life you deserve.

LEARN TO CLIMB HIGHER

There are many books written about money or better still successful life, search the internet, go to recommended bookshop or ask question from your parent, gather some useful information from them, dial into people testimonies by sharing their experience, you can also make an appointment with your citizen advice burro, your local bank manager can also be of many assistance by educating you on subject of money, the higher you can climb the better you can view the world, do not be lazy to study, God gave you your brain to study, read newspaper, watch educative programme on the television to acquire useful information that will provoke you to achieve your success.

To acquire money, you need to study. If you want to be a millionaire, you need to study the ways of millionaires.

7. VISION

" And it shall come to pass afterward that I will pour out My Spirit on all flesh; Your sons and your daughters shall prophesy, Your old men shall dream dreams, Your young men shall see visions. **JOEL 2:28**

Life could be meaningless without a vision making everything to fall aside, imagine the vehicles moving on the road without a traffic light or a traffic police directing the driver of the vehicles to their respective driver's direction, everything will be chaotic. Anybody could live a compromising a life when there is no vision, I have spoken to lot of people who told me they don't need money to survive their life and that if you have more money there will be much trouble, some people even believe that money will invite evil life styles and can make someone to denial the almighty God, what a pity, this are all lies of the money, the actual fact is that anybody can make any excuses especially when they have no vision to pursuit.

Your vision becomes a pain that set your motive on fire, encouraging you to hit the right target in life. *If you don't have a vision, you are like a blind man living on the edge of life*, but the vision in your heart will motivates you to acquire money.

MONEY IN YOUR VISION

Just like my own personal testimony, it was my vision that pioneer me to have interest for money, to my little understanding I thought money is not for everyone, if you are born rich you are okay to have more money and if you are not born rich then please never be comfortable to stay in that level. As a Christian with old school brought up I strongly believed that money is the root of all evil without checking the real bible passages which actually contradict this hollow philosophy of man, according to the bible *"The love of money is the root of evil."* Money plays an important role in our vision, before a city is build we need to consider the cost, no matter the types of vision money will help us to take it to another level, it will help us to expand the scope of our operation, money will broadcast your God's giving vision to the rest of the world and connect you to the right people. Every visionary have a mission to fulfill, they love to build sky scraper which can only be possible with the help of money.

YOU ARE NOT LIMITED

Most people are not up to the task of their vision due to lack of money, and this is why I said vision will lead to provocation of acquiring money Please do get me right, money on your vision is never a do or die affair, as long as what you receive is from God He will surely make a provision for your vision. The earth is still of the lord and the fullness thereof, He owns the cattle on the hill, God will make away where there seems to be no way. After all He is God of provider (Jehovah Jireh).Your vision will likely provoke you to acquire money, what so ever is laying in your heart without money you are limited, vision remains stagnant without money and when you see others excelling in their own vision anger is bound to pile up in your mind. This type of anger is not bad, all you have to do is to turn this acts to the position of acquiring money in any form as describe in this book.

8. THE WORD OF GOD.
Your word is a lamp to my feet and a light to my path.

Words play an important role in people's life, whenever there is darkness words will shell a light, words can either build or break you. Sometime life become meaningless if there is no spoken word. The situation get bemused, words will motivate you to do extra ordinary things. The word of God gives understanding. Every spoken word of God gives life.

The words of God are sharper than a two-edged sword. It penetrates into the bone marrow. Even if you are under a curse, the word penetrates into your life and cuts the curses. Try to study the word. The word of God is an eye-opener that shows you the right path to life. It moves you from poverty to the place of riches. Word will provoke you to do great exploits, Most of the time people feel comfortable in a situation they find themselves, for them to move to another level seem unfeasible, fear and disquiet grieve their lives which stops them from fulfilling their destiny. The only thing that can set such people free is a positive word of encouragement, word will transform you and push you to a place of glory, no matter what you are going through the word of God will give you comfort.

THE POWER TO MAKE WEALTH

Surprisingly many people due to their background are limited and have a little understanding about life; especially the issue of success is like a taboo. Many Christians believed they have to leave or die poor, if anybody possess riches among the brethren they will conclude the brother must be from the devil, but thank God for the word of God through motivated preachers in our generation that enlighten us about the need why Christian should be rich and still serving God, today with much searching through the Bible many people are now provoked and they search for the wealth. After all, the word of God say *I am the one who give you the power to make wealth.*

The word of God will provoke you to take your place in the competitive world. The more you know how to make things happen the better you chase after your right. People wish to take a step but if there is nobody to teach or show them how to do it they remain paralyzed. Whatever you want to be in this life the word of God is like a mirror that can help you to reflect your future, it's also like a fire that can burn your heart which will provoke you to action. After all, nobody can hold fire and remain silent. Fire will preserve you, refine you, shape you like gold which passes through the fire, you might have been through many challenges of life, the word of God will lift you up and show you the way forward, teaching you the basic principle of life and point you to the right direction.

114

For your information the word of God is an eyes opener, many people are blind toward their future, they are comfortable with poverty, enemies have taken over all their benefits in life but when the words of God are released just like an arrow it will penetrate to their heart immediately which will greatly provoke them to take action.

Do you know that the entire secret to unlock your prosperity is hiding inside the book called **THE BIBLE**. Stop staring at it just open and keep on reading until you find your purpose in life. Do you need money to fulfill your assignment? please read the Bible and meditate on it, you shall be like a tree planted by the river side which yields its fruit in his season and what so ever you do shall prosper and your leaves shall not wither.

Joshua one of the leaders in Israel concluded by saying *"do not let the word of God departs from your mouth, meditate on it day and night so that you may be careful to do what is written, then you shall prosper and have great success."*

GREAT PROMISES ARE HIDING INSIDE THE WORD OF GOD

Any time the word of God comes to you, you will never remain the same, the word will give you wisdom and understanding and the more you are enlightened the better you will perform; the word of God is so powerful, there is always reaction, *it has the capacity to perform with excellent result anywhere you send the word of God something will definitely happen* and your life will not be the same anymore, if you have not yet provoke with your sense of reason why not try the word of God you will realize your purpose in life and before you look any further you will see yourself climbing the ladder of wealth.

Nothing changes people's life better than the word of God because there lies the purpose of mankind, according to the bible we are made in the likeness of God and fivefold of dangerous blessing was pronounce on us by God himself Genesis 1:28 *(1). Fruitful (2) Multiply (3) Fill the earth (4) Subdue (5) Dominion.*

As long as you are made aware of all these promises, your eyes will be wide open to know wisdom in the secret place which will provoke you to do extra ordinary things and to acquire your desirable money, go ahead and search the necessary part of the word of God that point you to a wealthy place. It's your right don't let the devil rob you anymore, it's okay to get angry as long as you will end up acquiring your wealth and that is what I am talking about. Can somebody say amen to that?

9. YOUR ENEMY.

Life is full of many obstacles, challenges, trial, temptation and all sorts of things. Due to these factors lot of people are afraid of enemies which I classify as opponent. The truth of the matter is that enemies are nothing to be afraid of in life rather this is a stepping stone to help you to get to your place of assignment. Although enemy is not interesting in your progress, they will try all methods to block you from reaching your goals in life, their ferry hanger is so hot that can consume you in a wink of an eye, the enemy will push you to the place of your blessing it all depends on how you handle it.

As far as history is concerned, every successful people on earth will tell you the impact of their enemy which often lead or cause them to sit tight and focus until they arrive in the place of their glory.

OPPRESSION WILL MULTIPLY YOU.

You enemy can provoke you to acquire money to the point that, when their anger arose over your life by throwing a heavy stone in your life, the way they mock you or their kinds of oppression will definitely lead to your anger At these point, I want you to know that enemies are specialized in mocking people all what they are looking for is to destroy life and put obstruction but be confident of these. The more you are oppressed, the better you can multiply. Your enemy might have made a covenant that you are not going to make it in life, don't worry keep on moving all they are trying to do is to discourage you, never mind concentrate on your goal after all they are not your maker, look ahead and keep on doing what you know best and you will soon arrive in your place of assignment. It's just a matter of time.

You may have fallen or failed several times and the enemy keeps saying you cannot amount to anything in your life again, it's all lies keep moving on the drama is not over yet there is a second part, let the enemy anger provoke you to put more effort and try harder it's just a matter of time you will soon arrive in your wealthy place.

SOARING IN THE MIDST OF ENEMIES

No matter what enemy/accuser might have done they are not meant to stop you but to provoke you to move ahead. The more your persecutors provoke you, the better are the chances you have to rise to the top.

King David the greatest king who ever lived was a perfect example, despite the increase and molestations of his accuser he was triumphant and made it to the top, he acquired wealth in his life time and left inheritance for his children. Joseph also was let down by his brothers who became enemy of progress by selling him to the foreign land Egypt hoping that Joseph dream of success will perish. At last he rise to the top and make history, you too can make it no matter what the accusation may look like, it's only take a fool to perish because of the enemy, no one can stop you except yourself, your life doesn't depend on others opinion. Whatever opposition you might face in life, remember the first people who invented the Air craft flying in the sky now was actually opposed by their own father who was a professor that claimed it is impossible for anything to fly on the sky except birds, did any other thing fly in the sky? Just think about it and be provoked by the limitation enemies may label on you.

10. EGO

Every human being is born with a living lion inside of them. Most of the times the lion may be sleeping and have no one to awake them but any time something stirs up the anger of the lion you will be amazed how the lion inside of you roars to motivate you and forcefully make things happen. The lion that resides inside of you is called an ego which can be referred to as self-esteem.

Without ego, everyone will settle for a comfortable life, some are comfortable with poverty by accepting their faith or blaming others for their unsuccessful life, but due to the ego, your mentality can be challenged and provoke you to acquire your desirable success.

NOT WHAT PEOPLE SAY THAT MATTERS BUT WHAT YOU SEE

A young school boy was sent home from school due to unpaid school fees, his parents were poor and could not afford the money and the boy was sent to borrow the money from his rich uncle. On getting there the uncle abused him vigorously, immediately the young boy left the uncle, the ego inside of him was provoked and later the young boy grew up to be one of the most successful people in life.

When others refuse to accept you, then you accept yourself. When others see you as a failure; your ego will rise up and reject that condemnation. The ego in you will refuse to sleep until something is been done.

Many years ago, when I was about to leave Germany, I had the opportunity of walking away with 95,000 Deutschmarks, but my ego refused to take such money because I believe that my future is more than that. I rejected what others consider to be the last chance.

There is ego that lives within you the power that works within you which can ignite your ability in performance just like the accelerator does in a motor car. Ego takes you to another level; stirs up the self confidence in you and shows you the way forward even in the midst of difficult situation, the ego inside of you will help you and lead you to a wealthy place.

WHERE IS YOUR EGO DRIVING YOU?

Your ego can also be described as personality, something that resides inside of you and gives you courage that it's going to be well, just like a roaring lion looking for food during hunger, nobody on earth can be successful unless the lion inside of them is awake, a sleeping giant will never amount to anything except if he is awake.

Take a look at almost the richest people on earth majority are from poor background, they are ordinary people, the ego in them provoked them to do the unusual which led them to their dream land, *ego will drive you higher and help you to acquire the money you want in life, everybody have an ego it's only depend on which direction they drive it,* whatsoever your ego pointed to will be the direction you move toward in life, when situation are not in desirable order your ego will motivate you till you are able to put situation in control, self-worth will show you how better you can perform even in the midst of scarcity, at times due to circumstances in life, people feel discouraged, losing all hope but the ego inside of you will fuel your body and put you back in tract until success is achieved.

There is no limit as to when you can become in life you can be a millionaire, own your bank or become financial freedom, you can be 120 yrs-old and the Lord still endow you with Billions of pounds, everything is hiding inside your mind and only ego will push it out.

SUMMARY OF THINGS THAT CAN PROVOKE PEOPLE TO AQUIRE MONEY

- THE DESIRE FOR MONEY IS FAR BEYOND IMAGINATION BUT RATHER PROVOCATION BUT WITHOUT A FLAME THERE IS NO FIRE (Having a dream of Money and waking to Reality)
- IF MONEY ANSWERS ALL THINGS WE SHOULD BE ANGRY AND OFFENDED THAT WE HAVE SOME QUESTION OF INADEQUECY THAT MAY NOT BE ANSWERED IN OUR LIFE. (*ECCL.10:19*)
- THERE IS NOTHING WRONG WITH BEING ANGRY IT WILL HELP YOU TO TAKE A NECESSARY STEP AND MOVE YOU TO THE NEXT LEVEL ESPECIALLY GOOD ANGER.(*MATT.5:6*)

THINGS THAT CAN PROVOKE
PEOPLE TO ACQUIRE MONEY

1. POVERTY. *DEUT 28:24 (POVERTY IS A CURSE- SOME ONE ELSE TAKING CREDIT FOR ALL THE HARD WORK YOU HAVE DONE)*
2. FAILURE *JUDGES - 6:1-14.*
3. CHALLENGES - *1CHRO.4:9-10 (YOU CAN SET A GOAL FROM YOUR PRESENT CHALLENGES IN LIFE.*
4. OPPORTUNITY- *2 KINGS 7:1-17 (OPPORTUNITY DOES NOT CARRY LABELS THEY ARE WRAPPED IN OUR DAILY HAPPENNINGS)*
5. HISTORY/BACKGROUND -*JUDGES 11:1 (THERE IS A STORY YOU CANNOT CHANGE BUT YOU CAN CHANGE YOUR CHARACTER, HABIT)*
6. STUDY- *2TIM.2:15.*
7. VISION -*GEN. 37:5 (YOUR VISION BECOME A PAIN THAT SET YOUR MOTIVE ON FIRE ENCOURAGING YOU TO HIT THE RIGHT TARGET IN LIFE)*
8. WORD OF GOD - *JOSHUA 1:8.*
9. ENEMIES *ECCL. 7:12* .
10. EGO. (SELF ESTEEM) THERE IS A POWER THAT WORKS WITHIN YOU WHICH IGNITES YOUR ABILITY IN PERFORMANCE. JUST LIKE A THROTTLE IN THE CAR.

CHAPTER EIGHT
THE IMPORTANCE OF MONEY

Money frees you from doing things you dislike. Since I dislike doing nearly everything, money is handy. Groucho Marx (1890 – 1977)

"For the LORD your God will bless you just as He promised you; you shall lend to many nations, but you shall not borrow; you shall reign over many nations, but they shall not reign over you. "If there is among you a poor man of your brethren, within any of the gates in your land which the LORD your God is giving you, you shall not harden your heart nor shut your hand from your poor brother, but you shall open your hand wide to him and willingly lent him sufficient for his need, whatever he needs. Beware lest there be a wicked thought in your heart, saying, 'the seventh year, the year off release, is at hand,' and your eye be evil against your poor brother and you give him nothing, and cry out to the LORD against you, and it becomes sin among you. You shall surely give to him, and your heart should not be grieved when you give to him, because for this thing the LORD your God will bless you in all your works and in all to which you put your hand. For the poor will never cease from the land; therefore I command you, saying, 'You shall open your hand wide to your brother, to your poor and your needy, in your land." Deut.15: 6 - 11

Money is so important that, lack of it brings problem, and too much of money will be a big headache. *Proverbs. 30: 8 - 9.* King Solomon said *"Give me neither poverty nor riches Feed me with the food allotted to me; lest I be full and deny You, And say, "Who is the LORD?" Or lest I be poor and steal, and profane the name of my God.*

No wonder some people run away from money issues because they don't want to have the kind of money that will make them deny God.

The reason I am writing the book on how to acquire Money is that I know in your heart that you love God and when money comes unto your hands, there are some things you will do for God. You need money so that you can serve your God faithfully.

If money is not important, then why are we working? Why do you buy clothing or want to look good? If money is not important, you will not be able to have the Bible. Some people printed the Bible and gave people free of charge. However, the printer didn't do it free of charge, neither does the binding nor the paper were free. This means some people paid money for what other got for free. But I want to challenge you that God will move you from being a receiver to a giver.

GIVERS NEVER LACK

The Bible says *"It is much profitable to give than to receive"* because the hand of he that receives is down while giver hand is always on top. King Solomon asked for wisdom to rule his people but God gave him money, on top of what he requested for. **1Kings3:12-13**.

Why will God give Solomon money? God knew that Solomon would need both. No matter how much your wisdom is, if you do not have money you amount to nothing. I mentioned earlier that wisdom gives you anointing but anointing without money turns to Annoyance. How will you feel if you are invited to a fundraising event but you cannot perform financially, of course you will be disappointed.

MONEY PLAYS IMPORTANT ROLES IN OUR SOCIETY FOR THE FOLLOWING REASONS.

1. FOR GOODS AND SERVICES

Have you been to the market environment and notice all the activities of what is taking place, the styles of setting up in business atmosphere, decorations, the products types, negotiations and all kinds of transactions all these are with the help of money. In the past years people used to trade by barter (the process of exchanging goods for goods) this procedure was a big confusion due to the ineffective ways of its operation, sometime you need meat and all others got will be similar thing or out of your need. When the use of money was introduced, the system of legal tender became effective and up till now you can go to market and place a demand for anything, with money you never lack anything. Money is portable, it could be fixed in your pocket, with today technology money is debited or credited into plastic cards called credit cards which allow you to trade effectively, people can exchange business on the internet without being seen face to face. Cheque also is another means of transaction which makes money the most important thing in our planet.

MONEY IS THE MEANS OF EXCHANGE

Everybody needs money for one thing or the other after all the food you eat does not come free. Though you may not pay for the land being used to plant/generate the crops that you eat but you need money to transport these items from the farm to the market. You need money to establish most things in life; you need money for goods and services, to buy and to sell. You need money to exchange for the things you do not have. You need money to pay for your house rent, school fees, and clothing. All your household utilities providers can only supply you with their services only if money is available. Every year new latest technologies are coming out, sometimes ago people are using black and white television, later color television came with big back that occupy a lot of spaces, but now a day the latest technology just develop a plasma television with a flat screen and all these thing are products of money.

Many businesses started very small and later develop to mega business such as Tesco supermarket selling farm products when they started, today the market has developed to selling of clothing, insurance policies and to sell many other thing. The road is full of latest cars while the sky is also full of different kinds of airplanes and to purchase all these goods you need money. If money is in your hand, heaven is the limit. You can afford anything in life, book holidays anywhere in the whole world, your children can attend whatever school they love. Money is important as people need it to buy goods and pay for services.

2. TO HELP THE POOR AND THE NEEDY

The society we live nowadays, despite the great increase in wealth as recorded more than the olden days, people are becoming poorer. There are wealthy people around but others are living in the absolutely poverty. Few people are eating the national cakes while others are crying looking for assistance. Many have left their native land in search of greener pastures. Some travelled across the land others across the Atlantic Ocean, migrating to foreign land all for the sake of help and adequate care. The little they have is never enough as family and friend are depending on them to survive. To make the matter worse, there are current wars all around the world and the natural disasters are disrupting our planet such as tsunami, volcanic eruptions, hurricane Katrina in America, the Hattie earthquake etc. all of these have contributed to the downfall of many people which makes them seek for help. The bible says he *that lend to the poor have giving to the Lord.*

The duty of every God fearing people is to help the poor and the needy, the bible encourage us never to turn away from helping especially our own blood. How many times have you received request for assistance from your relatives back home, for their needs and you turned them down?

SOMEONE NEEDS YOUR HELP

A lot of people depend on you, especially those people who found their way to Europe. You are their hope. Whenever they want to get married or want to solve some important issues, they wait on you for their hope. They are always looking forward to receiving from you. This is why the first phone call you receive from home is not about them knowing how well you are doing but how badly they need your help. May God give you money to help those people. There are people on the street who don't even have a roof on their heads. And they are waiting for your help.

How will you feel with your bible, your grammar, your speaking in tongue, and someone walk to you asking for £10, and you tell that person of, by doing that, you have just defiled your religion. A true Christian should be able to help the needy. How long ago have you had a thought of shopping for your neighbor?

GIVING TO CHARITY

There are so many charitable organizations that need your help such as Cancer Research, Heart Foundations, apple of nations etc.; they want every penny from you. The more you help people in need the better our society, many people are waiting on you to survive. Whatever you donate makes a huge difference and it goes a long way Thank God for some rich people in the society who are extending their generosity to the charity organization which make research possible by preventing further disaster and putting an end to some deadly diseases that can wipe away our entire generation.

Deut.15:11 "for the poor shall not cease out of the land: therefore I command you saying, thou shall open your hand wide unto your brother, to the poor, and to the needy, in thy land".

The money God gave to you is not just for your benefit only, you are trusted to share with others in need that doesn't have the privileges you have, they are looking up to you in time of needs and they are not interested in your story of excuses. I see God transforming you from that same story of excuses all years round to a better situation, in Jesus' name.

3. TO LIVE A BETTER LIFESTYLE.

The rich rules over the poor, And the borrower is servant to the lender.

Proverbs 22:7 To my surprise I have seen people in the continent of Europe; some citizens are living under a very bad condition. Some live like animals in the zoo. People living in the jungle are even better than some of these people. Imaging with the entire programme and planning the government put in places and the huge benefits provided for the people some still live from hand to mouth. You need money to live a better life which includes better educational system not just going to school anyhow but a better private school with the best teachers who can influence the performance of your children to have brighter future. Some children have disability in brain; they have low understanding in learning, they cannot even spell out their name; such students need private tutors. With the help of money you can employ a better teacher in order to impact some basic knowledge in them.

YOU CAN HAVE IT IF YOU REALY WANT IT

According to the history of Richard Branson the owner of virgin airline, he had some disability in learning during his school period and with the help of a private tutor today, he is blessed and lives a better life. No wonder the man is giving too much money to found better education for children with disability learning.

In the absence of money you only use any common resources, no wonder some people enroll their children in public/general schools, where they learn how to take drugs, graduate to be jobless, some ending up to become a liability to the society.

To have a better life means you are making use of all the opportunities available for you in life. You don't just manage resources but make use of the best, giving the best to yourself and help others to fulfill their assignment, you are not living because you exist but having better quality in the means of quantities, better services and great life.

People around giving you the best you deserve, you are loved and respected by people, sleeping in the comfort of your home with all facilities around you, taking family holiday to your heart's desire, eating the best food, having nothing to worry when it comes to spending, you can shop at any supermarket without worry.

NOT JUST THE REMNANT BUT THE BEST

I remember a documentary of the late pop star Michael Jackson shown on TV, he visited a shop to buy some nice expensive stuff. First and foremost, the whole shopping centre was closed down because of the security for an hour before the legend appeared. He immediately entered the shop. Michael Jackson was just pointing to some items which were very expensive- about $100,000 each. "I need 6 of this, 8 of that, 12 of the others over there and so on and so forth," he said. When you have money you are in total control, money is powerful no wonder some people will do anything to make money.

The benefit of life is to enjoy it and live it to the maximum as King Solomon put it in the bible *"Live joyfully with the wife whom you love all the days of the life of your vanity, which he has given you under the sun, all the days of your vanity"* **Ecclesiastes 9:9**

Do you know that when you are rich, life is a lot safer than when you are poor? A poor man wouldn't want to take an airplane for a journey unless it's an international journey, even at that, he would be bargaining for a second class or economy flight. I pray that from today, you will not fly in economy class but in first class, in Jesus' name. You also need to know that when you are rich, people give more to you, whereas in poverty even your best friends deny you. I see God changing your lifestyle.

NEVER STAY TOO SMALL

What is the challenge of life, if you have to wait until others got the best and you are lining up for the remnant all the days of your life, struggling to meet a living, imagine some parent searching for the cheapest pampers for their child's usage, scavenging for the cheapest sales all about the city, looking for "buy one get one free" going to charity shop to buy used items for their family what a life? Please don't get me wrong there is no crime in little beginning a time when thing are not right you can help yourself by cutting your cloth according to your size but staying long in this kind of situation is an abomination before your creator and remember this is not what God has in stock for you and your children if others can enjoy a better lifestyle, it's also possible for you too.

4. TO FULFIL YOUR DREAMS AND VISION

There are many people with great visions and dreams that are big enough to brighten our generation, people with stunning ideas whom God has gifted with extra ordinary knowledge, all these things Cannot just establish with ordinary words of mouth, you need money to materialize them.

Recently we started a new Face of Our God given vision in London, called Praisetek Light Club. We now operate the club regularly, to fulfill the visions. It all began, while I was a young boy I got a revelation to set up a Christian clubhouse. Where believers children will be able to gather together dance and listen to good music without swearing, lifting their holy hands by praising God. The admission is totally free so as to allow non-believers to also attend the event; you should have known that doing this didn't come for free, the venue, leaflets, advertisements and all the likes' costs money.

Many people have dreams/visions to do one thing or the orders, with the help of money everything will come to life, money will allow you to take your ideas to another level. Without money your dream could be jeopardized and if care is not taken, they could be abolished, money will make your dream look exceptional, vision will be highly inspired by the help of money. You may be operating on a low profile due to inadequate of money, but as soon as your hand grabs money, there will be a turn around with great transformation, money in your vision is heavenly taste, you will be amazed what money can do in that dream or vision in your mind.

Please be encouraged, when God gives you vision He will definitely make a provision, you don't have to have money when it come to God's revelation, what you need is total obedience and faith which will lead to implementation. Although some time your vision may seem tarry or delay you just have to wait for it, God will surely make away. Every vision is subject to an appointed time. For further explanation on how to fulfill your God's giving vision /dream without money you can order for my book titled "*GRAB YOUR OPPORTUNITY*" an insight to this subject.

YOUR DREAM CAN BE WEIGHT ON THE SCALE OF MONEY

Money is very important in the life of visionary; it will shine light and give understanding. Money will help you to expand your vision to the wider world, what so ever you want to do money will create an exposure, evangelize your brands and connect you to others who can also be of an assistance in the vehicles of your dream/vision.

Some people have a dream to preach on the television as an evangelist with a great message of hope to the hopeless, without money everything will be a dream of the mind.

MERCY SHIP ON THE MOVE

I heard of a vision called mercy ship where professional doctors travelled by sea inside the ship to different countries of the world in order to help people in need, sometime six months these good Samaritans have to be on the ocean, rendering solution to the affected by giving them medical cares, all these thing cost money.

Have you ever been to some churches and see the way the sanctuaries are fully decorated, people worship God in the beautiful environment, the styles of their music will lead you to the presence of God without struggling. You will never know how creative people are until their hand touch money. Money has helped to improve infrastructural projects and add peace of mind. Disney World could not look fantastic if not for the sake of money, Coca-Cola may not be widely available if money was not present. Money will help you to define your dream; the government is changing the looks of our streets yearly due to the budget of money available by the tax payer. If you travel to the Asian countries you will see what impact money has played over there to build their cities. I can go on and on just to tell you how money plays an important role in your dreams/vision.

I know there are dreams in your hearts. Some of you want to erect skyscrapers, mansions, develop the old city, make this world a better place and put smiles on people faces all these don't come free. This is why I said; surely you need money to accomplish those dreams and visions of yours.

5. MONEY PLACES YOU ON TOP

We all have a desire as individual on this planet called the earth, everybody aspires to be great, do something extraordinary. Nobody want to be on the bottom, we just like to be on top and be in control of everything- be it finances, position, family etc, people dream big and love to take positions although it is never a crime as this is the desire of God to all mankind as spoken by God in the foundation of the earth **Genesis 1:26- 28** "*Be fruitful and multiply, take dominion, rule over.*

With this glorious prophecy everyone wants to climb higher and map on wings like a dove. What so ever is your field, everybody aim higher, you just cannot be comfortable with your level, but can I tell you if all these desires are on you but without money these will only be wishes. Money will take you from the low level to the top, *the more you have the better you are in procession*, even if you are the youngest of your family, or worse still born with disabilities, so far money come to your hand, all the final conclusion of the family affair is in your care, no one take any decision without your approval.

MONEY WILL PUT YOU ON A MAP

Nobody respects poor man. When people are poor, they are poor indeed, but when a rich person arrives at a place, he is rightly recognized. Even the way they dress, from top to toe, people recognize that someone has just arrived, they are well respected and given the best seat during a ceremony. No one has regard for a poor man who is full of ideas but with no money. Nobody wants to listen to their advice. You need money to be able to stay on top. It will make people to respect you. Some people whom you don't like but for the fact that they have what it takes for people to like them (MONEY) you don't have any alternative but to like them.

Many cities of the world that are now highly visited by tourists used to be no- go zones but money has placed them on the priority list and allowed people to be hungry just to catch a glimpse of the land. When you have money, no-one talks to you anyhow, everybody wants to be your friends, they seek for your opinion before they embark on doing anything. You have to be number one on the priority list. If they're planning a program, and you have not chosen a date for them, they don't have any date in mind. Some ladies give out their body free of charge to a total stranger, not that they don't know what they want, but they think the man has what it takes to fill their stomach and to fulfill their lustful desire which war against their flesh. No wonder some ladies have opened up their life-gate, for the king of evil to come in. Who is this evil king? Unwanted pregnancy, frustration, stress, terminal diseases, aids etc. May God deliver his people from all evil.

6. CREATING INHERITANCE FOR YOUR CHILDREN:

The Bible says *"A good man leaves inheritance for his children's children." Prov.13:22* there are three seasons in life, namely morning of life (Between 0-25 years of age) this is when you are born and started learning about life, a period where you depend on your parents to do everything in life, most especially to go to the best school, choose the best lifestyles and learn the moral of the family, study the culture or settle for the best of life. Everybody loves this period because they are just arriving, very innocent carefree, nothing to lose but much to gain. The period I called the reality of life where you have to settle for your own life, start a new family and get to know that life is not as you think.

Secondly the afternoon of life (Between 25-50 years of age) where whatsoever you do is no longer a dream but reality. This is the period people works hard to cater for their own family and prepare for the next season of life.

The third season of life (Between 50 years upward) this is the final season of a man on Earth, where you have to carefully give account of what you have come to do on earth, a period where no more excuses' will be taken. What so ever you do at this period is for the benefit of the coming generation, and when you depart from the surface of the earth what so ever you have labored for become the benefit of your children and children to come. *The dream of every child is to have a good foundation where they can be building on*.

People inheritance is weight in the scale of money, the more you have the better is for your children, after all our prayer is to see our children having the best life more than the parents and this is what money will do as long as you have more than enough that will brighten the future. .

BE CAREFUL OF THE BAGGAGE YOU LEAVE BEHIND

What are you leaving behind for your children? I hope is not your cut-of jeans, drop-down trousers, Cannabis, abnormal social misconducts or whatsoever. You may think you've inspired that your child for now but, with these irresponsible actions it's dangerous. Just imagine in the future, your child asks for money but all you could say is, you don't have money just like your normal excuse in the past. The child will see you as an irresponsible father. And that is who you are frankly. In other words, you need money to create an inheritance for your children, that even after you might have departed from this world, your children will say, thank God for our parent.

If it happens that you die today, what will your children say about your financial situation "Thank God for our parent for leaving this inheritance for us?"

There are many generals who left everlasting inheritance for their children in our generation, such as Coca-Cola, Thomas Edison, JF Kennedy, Mercedes Benz, liver brother, etc. These people's families will ever be grateful in life for the inheritance their parents left behind.

PLEASE STEP CAREFULLY

However, I need to balance my teachings, I know because of all the above examples of cloud of witnesses some of the youth might want to go to the path of trafficking in drugs or steal, in other to meet up with life. NO. Please don't do that, the future is still more ahead of you than any past recorded failure, you are not a failure until you quit trying, as long as there is life there is hope, you only have to make it swift while the sun still shines.

I have already explained from the beginning and you should know that those evil thinking is just one out of the 10ways of making money which I called DUBIOUS WAY. Dubious wealth will never last long. If you traffic in drugs to make money, you are joking. you will soon be caught. It might take 6 to 7years if at all for you to be caught, but your waterloo will surely come. Please don't go there. Wait for your time. Use the wisdom I have taught in this book to acquire your own money.

7. TO SHOW THE GLORY OF GOD

God has a name to protect, and part of that name is "*I AM that I AM.*" The Bible says the cattle on the hill belong to Him. Our God owns the silver and gold, the desire of God is to give us wealth so that His Glory can be revealed in our life. *It is the desire of God to make you prosper.*" God is looking for a *signboard* to show His Glory. God has a Glory to show. Take a look at the sun; this is some of the Glory of God, the fishes in the oceans, the birds flying high in the sky, animals in the bush, the valleys and the mountains all these are part of the glory of God to show how splendor is the Lord most high. God did not create anybody on this world for nothing. God wants to make you a financial guru to show the world He is your Jehovah Jireh (the Lord that provides). He is looking for somebody that He can entrust with money. May the Lord make you a signpost to show the Glory of His power. Nobody like to serve a poor God, imagine stepping out of your luxurious car with Rolex watch in your hand, seeing a group of people around and you decided to witness Jesus Christ even before you say may Lord bless you, they will cheerfully respond to you because they can see the glory of God shining upon you. So you need money to show the glory of God.

DOING THE UNUSUAL FOR A BETTER RESULT

Matthew 14:15-21 This chapter talked about how Jesus fed 5000 people. The moral is, that you can respond to people's need as a Christian. To take gospel to the nation, you don't necessary have to shout or make noises before people accept the faith, the best form of spreading Christianity is to take care of people needs.

I know of a pastor who prepares five star breakfast for the homeless each morning and majority of people are coming to the Lord every day, some have open hospital for free medical cares, others operate educational system, supporting the communities projects. As a Christian you need money to show the world how glorious is our God.

FROM CRACK TO CHRIST

There was a particular story of a sister who was on drugs and prostitution for over five years on the street where my office is located in London. One day she walked into my office and demanded for money, actually I knew she was on drug due to her look and dressing.

I was speaking to her about Christ love, she will not listen to me, all she was demanding for was "Can I have the money please". The Holy Spirit ministered to my heart to give her the money and to my surprise she later gave her life to Jesus Christ and became my daughter in Christ. During her testimony she confessed that it was the money I gave to her that convinced her to finally surrender unto the lord. Today the lady is serving the Lord faithfully, even joined the choir, started working and paying tithes to the church, God is using her to win souls to the Lord and she is a gift to the body of Christ.

There are many stories in the bible relating to people who are very rich and serving God faithfully showing the glory of God, such as Abraham, Jacob, Isaac, Solomon etc. in the Old Testament, also in New Testament - Cornelius, Joseph the Arimathaea one of the disciples who buried Jesus in his tomb and the Lord Jesus Christ himself according to the gospel.

CHRIST BECAME POOR FOR YOU TO BE RICH

The scale has been removed, you can operate in the power of your God; fulfill your God given- assignment without depending on lottery money to finance your projects. I pray you will not perish for lack of understanding which is eating some of our Christian believers whom Satan is still holding captives through their wrong mentality that a Christians need to be poor before they can enter the kingdom of God.

As from today, the God of Glory will make you to do exceedingly above all that you can imagine according to the power that works inside of you. God makes you rich and blesses you to be feeding the poor on the street, your house will become a place where people come to take money, The Lord will turn your house into a Social benefit office where friends and relatives will line up to take their benefits in Jesus' name I pray. Amen.

8. EMPOWERMENT AGAINST THE ENEMIES.

"Wisdom is a defense as money is also a defense" Ecclest.7:1

Every year, each country reserves a huge amount of money for the ministry of defense, a lot of money are been spent on training the militaries, Air forces, navies, the police forces. You will be surprised to know how much money is pumped into the judiciary department in order to allow peace and harmony in our society, the money spent on foreign policies, buying of equipment to prepare against the enemy is more than the money spent on health or the social system. Without money you are liable to an attack either the enemy within or outside.

Recently in United Kingdom and in America the citizens are complaining against the troops sent to Iran and Afghanistan to combat the Taliban by fighting war against the people who are terrorizing the westerners, many are complaining about the money spent on the soldiers and the equipment being too much. A lot of human right campaign against the government reaction demanded that the war should stop; actually the government has no choice other than to send more troops into these areas for the protections of the people because of the atrocity coming from those regions.

MONEY WILL FIGHT YOUR BATTLES

You need money to defend yourself against the war of poverty, with so many diseases in town. Adequate money will provide a good medical care, in part of African continent HIV/Aids are killing people rapidly and if care is not taken, the whole continent can be wiped out due to these epidemics. If you have money you can hire the best doctor to offer you good treatment, you can fight for justice by hiring the best barrister to defend you in the law court.

MONEY WILL RAISE A STANDARD

Different circumstances usually enfold individual life. Society may reject certain people, even their families may not want to see their faces. Just acquire money and see how your enemies will become your friends; money will help you to unveil the secret of your enemy.

People will become your informant and help you to fight any one that wages war against you as long as there is money in your pocket. You can hire the best security company to secure your family against crime.

Do you know that it was money they used to hang Jesus on the cross? They paid "30 shillings" to someone who is very close to Jesus so as to betray Him. People are wicked.

The Bible says "deliver us from all evil". When money is in your hands, you can buy the heart of anybody. If your neighbor hates you, just find a way of giving some money into his/her life, the story will change immediately. Money will defend you against enemy attack. When the enemy comes like a flood, money helps you to raise standard. You need money to defend yourself against unwanted situations.

9. MONEY IS USED TO FINANCE THE GOSPEL. *2Corin.9: 8-13*

Salvation is free but the tool to preach salvation is not free. You have heard the saying by some people that all the church needs is their money. But you should ask such people, why they go to the hotel and pay as much as £150 per night just to sleep on a bed. Why weren't they given the place free of charge because they have their own 3- bedroom house which they already paid monthly rent? Do they know the buildings most Churches use for services are not free? Some pastors have to pay through their noise before service can be held. As we have some complainers so we also have some genuine people who love to finance the gospel, so God has no choice but to give such people money in order to finance His Gospel. I see God giving you money to finance the Gospel of Jesus Christ, to organize crusades, pay for ministers' accommodation. God knows what you need.

The Bible says *for your Heavenly Father knows your need*. The truth is, if you properly position yourself in the sight of God he is able to make things happen for you financially, **seek ye first the kingdom of God and its righteousness and all other things shall be added unto you.**

CAN YOU BE TRUSTED?

The only people God will entrust with money in this generation are the generous people. The Lord is tired of people who spend money pointlessly. I know some of people are begging God for million pounds, but what have they done with the £100 He entrusted with them. Some of you don't stay home as soon as you are with just ordinary £100; all you do is patronizing West-End, gambling, raven. Some people just with ordinary £1000 in their pocket, their wife can't see them at home anymore; everything in their system will change, no time to pray as usual, even fellowship will be cut off, no wonder it's impossible for God to trust them with £10,000 according to their prayer request.

Ironically, sometimes we play over God's intelligence by our reaction. For example, He gave you £100, you couldn't pay your tithe of just £10 out of it. If this amount is so big for you to give as tithe to God who gave you a job, how would you want God to entrust you with huge amount of money?

Now you are saying that He knows your heart. Simply because you don't earn enough were the reason for not giving tithe. Do you think God is a fool? If you cannot be trusted with little, the Lord won't trust you with so much you are asking from Him. The Lord is waiting for you, until you are able to demonstrate faithfulness before God can open the wider door of money.

CAN YOUR ATTITUDE IMPRESS GOD?

The first thing I will love you to do is change your attitude towards giving. When you give, don't grumble, be happy, and support the good work of God. The almighty God doesn't forget the labor of our love, As long as you serve Him, He will bless you and grant you access to his wealth, make you to be rich and entrust you with the money of this world. God purposely bless some people because of the way they are reasoning with the works of the Lord. If God knows that you are going to support his works definitely your heaven will be open and you will be blessed far beyond people's imagination.

MONEY ATTRACTS MONEY

When there is money in the ministry, there will be transformation, everything will be done in decency and in order. In fact the more money in your ministry the better you attract rich people because money begets money, ministry can operate effectively, you can hire the best specialist in town, acquire more properties to allocate for your ministry.

If there are things needed more in the gospel, after the Holy Spirit and your anointing, you need money as a tool to drive the gospel to another level and according to the saying *"Anointing without money will result to annoyance"* may God bless you with money to take gospel to another level.

10. MONEY ANSWERS ALL QUESTIONS

A feast is made for laughter, and wine makes merry; but money answers everything Eccles.10:19

If there is no question definitely there will not be any answer. I mentioned earlier, that if money answered all things, there are questions and situations in our life which we are yet resolved, I don't know what's in your heart; neither do I know the visions that you do have nor your plans, but the *Bible says many are the plans in man's heart but God will make it happen*. There are things in our mind that bargain for money, I pray the Lord will surely make it happen.

IT'S POSSIBLE TO BE LIKE PRESIDENT OBAMA

Some of you have it at the back of your mind to do great things. Some want to become President of a nation. Obama did not get to be the President of America simply because he is a Black man, not at all. He got to the position because of wisdom and with money from people who financed his electoral campaign. I see God changing your situation, transforming your life. I see God bringing you into the place of your fulfillment. I see you entering into the place of wealth.

Right now, you might be going through tough seasons, life may be unfair on you, what so ever you see either failure or rejection, you have tried everything-still nothing is working, please keep on trying and hold on for it's a matter of time. Never give up; you are just a little bit closer to your breakthrough. Do you know when a pregnant woman is very close to delivery, the pain usually increases. That is what is going on right now, your miracle is on the way that is the reason God ordered me to write this book for people like you to read.

As a prophet of God, I am convinced your tears have gone to the Lord. He will send you a helper of destiny and your windows of heaven will soon be open. When a situation is like this, please stop complaining, give God the praise, follow all the necessary instructions as written in this book and be expectant your miracles are on the way, every question in your heart will be answered and you will fulfill your dreams / visions not long from now.

PRAYER

Lift up your hands and pray to God now. Lord I need money to fulfill all righteousness in my heart, to sponsor the gospel, to do great explorations, to do extra ordinary things. Lord I call unto you, who knows everything. You created me in my mother's womb; you are the one who gave me power to make wealth. Today Lord, I ask of you to give me money that will make me important, indispensable, to bless your name. The lord shall supply all my needs according to his riches in glory through Christ our lord. All these are asked in the precious blood of Jesus Christ, my provider. (Amen)

THE SUMMARY OF THE ESSENTIAL OF MONEY

- *MONEY IS VERY IMPORTANT THAT IF YOU DONOT HAVE IT THERE WILL BE PROBLEM AND TOO MUCH MONEY WILL BE A BIG HEADACHE –PROVERBS 30:8-9.*
- *KING SOLOMON THE GREATEST KING WHO EVER LIVED ASKED FOR WISDOM TO RULE HIS PEOPLE BUT GOD GRANTED HIM MONEY MORE THAN HIS WISHES IN LIFE. -1 KING.3:12-13.*

WHY DO WE NEED MONEY

1. FOR GOODS AND SERVICES - *GEN.23:13; EZRA 7:17.*
2. TO HELP THE POOR & NEEDY - *DEUT.15:10-11.*
3. LIVE A BETTER LIFE STYLE - *PRO.22:7.*
4. FULFILL YOUR DREAM /VISION -*LUKE 1 4:28.*
5. PLACE YOU ON TOP. -*PRO.19:4.*
6. CREATE AN INHERITANCE FOR CHILDREN- *PRO.13:22.*
7. TO SHOW THE GLORY OF GOD - *MATT.14:15-21.*
8. EMPOWERMENT AGAINST ENEMIES - *ECCL.7-12.*
9. TO FINANCE THE GOSPEL. - *2 CORIN.9:8-13.*
10. HELP YOU TO ANSWER ALL THINGS- *ECCL.10:19.*

CHAPTER NINE
THE LOGIC OF MONEY

Save a little money each month and at the end of the year you'll be surprised at how little you have. Ernest Haskins

<u>Mathew 25:14-29.</u>

What is logic? The philosophical theory of reasoning. It is the branch of philosophy that deals with the theory of deductive and inductive, argument and aims to distinguish good reasoning from bad ones.

The system on how money works is this. Millionaires talk about Ideas, average people will talk about things and small people will talk about other people. When you see people gossip, it's because they are poor. A rich man doesn't gossips. When they do that, they gossip about ideas. An average man doesn't gossip about ideas or people, but they talk about things. ***The way you think will determine how you can make money***. A poor- minded person has nothing to talk about than other people's matters {Gossiping about their personality, what he/she wears etc.} But a rich person is thinking; how they can produce something special and at the same time make money out of that. An average man's mentality is to look for someone who can produce special thing, instead of thinking of how he can go out and make his wealth by producing the special thing himself. Whosoever that speaks to you, try to identify your areas of mentality because money begets money. Like a pregnant woman, when you conceive what you give birth to is a baby.

How does logic work?
1. YOU NEED TO WORK FOR MONEY.

You need to get a job and earn income for you to make money. Working enables you to go out in the day, and return back home with a form of remuneration which makes you going. Traditionally, majority of the world population are in this category.

The Bible supported this *"He that does not work must not eat."* **2 Thess. 3:10**

Money will not come to you unless you are doing something.

You need to get a job, in order not to stay idle, the employee are the working force; very diligent in what they are doing so that they don't have to depend from hands to mouth, but depending on income. Work will pave way for many things, a community where there is no work, rate of crime increases. Idleness is a criminal offence before the Lord. An idle mind is the devil workshop. Anybody who is not doing anything will be liable to think evil and carry it out which will become harmful to people around them.

When you are busy or go somewhere every day {employed}, then you know something is about to happen. That's why in every developed country, they pay attention to every working person, because they are the ones that move the economics of the nation forward.

MORE WORKERS BETTER SITUATIONS

The bible says *As my father is working, I also need to work.*

Jesus didn't just come to earth and preach salvation, he was working. He stayed with his earthly father for 30years, learning carpentry.

I have seen some Christians, who resigned from their jobs, doing nothing, depending on the fact Jesus is coming soon. No wonder they look shattered and poor. The logic of money demanded that until your hand does something before you can acquire money, when you work, you are able to support your family and also contribute to the tax system which enables the government to carry out the task for the state or country, The more a country have people in the working class the better is their economy.

Today some countries are developed due to the increase in their working forces. When citizens develop the mentality of labor forces, circumstances change and life become enjoyable. When you stop working you stop earning. Money comes to those who work. If you are broke, get a job and money will start looking for you. The book of **Eccl.** Said *what so ever your hand find doing do it better*, life is too short for you to stay without doing something. Society depends on the working class to support the unemployed, people with disabilities and people of old age in the community. Job will put food on your table and add value to your life, when you work, financial institutions can trust you with borrowing, the government can also recognize you through the tax system and you can be elected or voted for during political era or do much more for your generation.

2. YOU NEED TO SAVE MONEY.

As long as you work and earn money either by monthly or weekly, you need to save money, because money begets money. Sad enough majority of parent do not teach their children on how to save money and today the mentality of people is just to get the money lavish it on pleasure, travel to places, buy expensive cars, take friends to different hotels, give them five star treatment just to know they have arrived. This is wrong mind set, you need to save money. If money is made to be spent, how do you get it back?

As I said earlier on money has wings {it flies}, it is also a spirit, {it vanishes}. These are the challenges why some people have not yet become millionaires.

For your information do you know that if you can save all the money you have been spending unnecessarily over the years or should be deposited into saving, imagine how buoyant your finances would be by now. You need to save money which I termed Banking System. **Mathew 25:27.** Says ***"So you ought to have deposited my money with the bankers, and at my coming I would have received back my own with interest."***

There is business account, current account, savings account, ISA, fixed deposit accounts etc. there are many ways of saving money, go and find out from the bankers.

HABIT CAN BE DEVELOPED

Talking about saving, I remember a master while in school. He was a "Chain-smoker". He always bought a lot of cigarette packs, he smoked half of the stick and put the remaining half under his bed. So by the middle of the month when he becomes broke, he goes back to those half cigarettes. These he takes till the end of the month when he gets salary again. By so doing, he was able to keep his mouth running with his smoking. And I said to myself that this idea could be transformed and turn it to something special.

I adopted this logic instead of cigarette, I started saving some coins from my left over during money surplus under my bed and surprisingly, I have accounted for over £900 in total. This analogy could be used in getting acquainted with the logic of saving. There are many ways you can save. Do you know that, the cup of coffee you take every morning, you can discipline yourself by staying away from it. Take water instead and save that £1? If you are able to do that on a daily basis for so many years, think of how much you will realize. There are so many ways that you can save. So don't let your mind deceive you that until you have millions of pound before you can be able to save. *If you cannot be disciplined when you have £10, you will never be disciplined when you have thousands of pounds.*

As the bible says "*he that is not faithful in little can never be trusted in much.* You need to save money because a day of need will arise. A wise man saves in the day of plenty, because life is seasonal. Look for smart way of saving and never cultivate the habit of eating mentality which make a lot of people become stranded in time of need.

they blame others for their lack instead of preparing for rain during drying season. People may not be able to give you money in difficult situation, but the little money you put in the saving will play an important role during dry season. A little there a little here will eventually become a mighty rock and before people can give to you they want to know how much you have at hand.

3. YOU NEED TO INVEST.

After you have worked and derived money from your labor, you also save some money which enables you to engage in business of your choices. If you have saved, your mind can move from just working to the starting of your own business. Why don't you start your own business? You have been working for certain length of time in a company. Have you not gained experience enough for you to start your own business? Starting a business is not as tough as some people think; you can start any business by turning what you know how to do best-This could be in time of hubby, talent, ideas or what so ever. Stop being deceived, you can turn whatsoever you do into business opportunity and make money of your dream.

As a Christian you are a child of promise, child of authority, with a covenant. God has made a covenant with you and your fore-fathers, that He will bless you. This blessing works when you start your own business. If you don't start your business as a Christian, you are telling God to bless your boss before blessing you. Actually when you have your business it's easier for God to operate fully in your business by releasing His full blessing upon your life. Some Christians say they can't serve God better, this is because they are under control of people. They cannot go to church regularly not because of sickness but they are under the supervision of their boss who dictates the time they can be allowed to attend church service.

When you have your own investment, you can be free to do whatever you love to do at your own privilege and nobody can control the way you spend your hours.

PUT YOUR MONEY TO WORK

The logistic of money warrant you to invest it wisely into any business venture, you can buy shares in company or speak to an expert who will be able to advise you on the best investment in town which will make you to be a shareholder in some company, you can also invest in housing market, you can buy houses through mortgage system, you can invest your money to anything that will produce you interest. Even if you are not good in investment you can seek business advice from your banker who will be able to assist you to put your money in some special business account that will yield interest and help you to make more money than just your traditional saving system.

Money is good when you put it to work, you don't just work for money, and rather your money should be working for you at all times.

The *only people who make more money are the one who allow money work for them*. Never let your money stay idle in your personal account or wherever you put your money, let it go out to the right place, invest it on a better ground for effective production. That is why you see the rich people still have more than enough.

The society are not aware about this, that is the more reason why only few discover this secret and make more money than the rest of people in the world.

TURNING YOUR TALENT INTO INVESTMENT

You do not need a million in your bank account before you can invest, investment can be done with very little in your hand, you need the right people to put you through, if I may shock you, a time you may not have money in your hand before you can invest, do you know that God has deposited something in your hand as a talent or dream which you can turn to an investment, it could be just a common ideas that come to your mind as I have explained in the previous chapter, all you have to do is to find a way of turning these thing to an investment so that you can start making money of your choice. You need to do something with the talent God gave you. If Eddie Murphy had stayed back in his room just like you are doing with your comedian activities now, who will hear about him?

Nothing stays forever, which is why you need to take your investment to another level when you are in business.

The talent God has given unto you; He doesn't want it to die. He wants you to do something. If you are a musician, record your album, after which you send it to the market. Don't just stays in recording. Write book on your album. Tell people 7 ways of singing a song. After which you tell them "the mistakes I made during my early stage in music". Yet they will buy it and by this you are taking your talent to another level and at the same time you can make more money.

4. YOU NEED TO SPEND MONEY.

When money comes to hand, you don't just save it, you also don't just invest it, but there is every need for you to also spend wisely. Don't spend like a prodigal son. Even in investment, there are downward and upward investments. Downward Investment is when you get money and rush to buy a car. If you are a car freak, you should know that after three months, if you decide to return or sell that car, it will never be worth the original price you got it initially. Spending money on clothes is also a downward investment; those designer things are all unnecessary spending that drains your purse. Treating yourself to the wildest of your dreams has never been a criminal offense. You can ride a nice cars, do whatever that your heart desires as long as you have invested and make money from your investment, you only need to spend wisely, shamefully some people buy car only to be begging people before they can fuel their car. You can buy a car, as long as it's going to be used as a means of making money. You can have a good "estate car" and obtain a license to use it as an airport pick-up/drop service, and still using it for personal stuff.

SPEND MONEY WITH EASY

There are holidays you need to go to. Enjoy yourself but don't go on holiday with loan from the bank because that is not wise or else, after coming back from the holiday you will pay with your blood. Don't just be carried away with saving money all the time, you need to find time to go to nice restaurants and treat yourself to nice things. I don't have any problem with you spending your money, but spend your money wisely!!! When you are spending, put up a smile. Don't let them know that you struggled to get it. Let them know that life is easy.

God created things in His own way and make things beautiful in His own time. Do you see the way sun shines, it doesn't struggle to shine. When the rain falls, it's with ease. You too don't need to struggle for life. Life is easy. Enjoy yourself to the maximum.

Money demands to be spent that is the purpose. When you spend money you put it to circulation and this will enable others to benefit. Money is call currency because it has the power to move round, everybody have access to it without exceptional as long as you use it for trading and services.

5. YOU NEED TO GIVE.

Stinginess is a sign of poverty, what is the significant of acquiring money and people around you could not benefit from your wealth, the logic of money demands that you should also give out for good purposes. If someone else doesn't release money to your hand how can you acquire it? Do not be greedy, you are not the only one who has worked hard for money, others had gone through even worse situations than what you have been through and they are still stretching their hand for the goodness of others.

The society values those who give money. And those who give tend to have more. Nobody will give you a contract no matter how many millions you have if you are not spending in that society. You need to sow it as a seed into people's life. Even in the church, God is the One who gives you power to make wealth, you need to pay your tithe faithfully. Learn how to give back to God; after all He gave you all the strength. You need to give money, don't just spend it on yourself or save or invest it.

DON'T ROB GOD. PLEASE DROP THE GUN

Do you know that sometimes people are too greedy? God gave you the job, made you not to be sick, and made you not to have accident, you wake up early in the morning, He only ask for just 10%. For your benefit, you are still complaining. All they need in the church is money. What a lame excuses.

Please don't be greedy. You need to pay your tithe as a Christian, and if you are not a Christian give offerings. *the Bible says in Luke 6:38 give and it shall be given back to you, good measure press down, shaken together, running over, so shall men give to your bosom.* If you are a type who gives people used cloth, shoes, household materials etc. Then be expecting to receive the same stuff as well but if you need money, you don't give any other thing than money. If you need happiness, you give happiness, if you need Love you have to give Love. If you need joy, you give out joy. *What you give is going to be what you get in a return that is another secret of life*.

You need to give alms to the poor not just giving to the church only. Go out and look for people in need so as to give to them. These are the secrets of millionaires.

Anybody you see that is prosperous, ask them their stories, they are crazy givers. And givers never lack. The reason some parents were able to leave things behind for children is because they were givers. So you need to give alms to the poor and give to charity. Most millionaires are setting aside so much money on a monthly basis for charity, because the prayers of the poor help them in their businesses. Recognize people who are there for you when things were not all right and those who help you on your way to the top, your friends, siblings, and anybody you can think of in your life, use money to appreciate then.

THE MOST IMPORTANT PEOPLE IN LIFE

Look after your parents because they are the source of your blessings as *the Bible says "honor your father and your mother so that your days will be long on earth.*

Don't let them die of poverty. No matter what any prophet says about your parents don't listen to them because your parents are the secret of your life. Without them, you don't exist. And if you starve them so shall you be starved of so many things, no matter how many billions you have. You also need to bless your mentors who sowed a seed of greatness into your life. There are people you dare not forget in your life, and if you really want to make money, you need to give money.

There is a woman in our ministry whom the Lord used me to prophecies to her life (To cook food for the less privileges on the street) to the glory of God she obeyed the instruction and did as the Lord said. Three days after, one of her daughters came from her homeland which they have seen for over twelve years to visit her, what a great surprised and in addition, the daughter's boss gave her £500 (five hundred pounds) as a gift.

THE FAR, FAITHFUL, FORTRESS AND THE FALLEN

You need to give to the **FAR**, those who are far away from you like your parents, your siblings, people that are abroad who have helped you in the journey of life by one thing or another. Send them gift by any means just to appreciate everything in your live and never allow distance to separate you. Extend your money to them so that God can remember you by sending you an angel from above.

You need to give to the **FAITHFUL.** Like your pastors, who are humbly teaching you things that will benefit your life, being who labor over you spiritual life by the seed of greatness he had sown to your life. Some people had paid a price for your lifted up, physically they may not give you money but the words of advice and courage they have spoken to your life which provoked you to take a step into your destiny. There are faithful grandmother who secretly pray you to your glory, the faithful wife who stood by you during unwanted situation, those sisters who were there for you when things were tough and much more.

You also need to remember the **FORTRESS.** There are people surrounded by strong hold, who are unfortunate because of things that befell on them, such as the less privileged, fatherless, orphans, the widow who doesn't have due to the death of her husband, the single parents, you need to help them. Don't look at them as people suffering, please give to them. Life is very delicate. Anything can go wrong at any time, nobody pray for tragic situation but it does happen Some people are not born with disability, it's just an accident that lead to such unpleasant situation and some are victims of circumstances. Please never write anybody off. They may be unfortunate or under stronghold for now but God owns their future, remember them with your money. Who knows what is in your own future, I do not pray that bad things happen to you but the more you give to the fortress the better God remember you and protect you from any tragedy to befall on you.

Lastly, you also need to give to the **FALLEN**. Those you know that are poor that cannot afford anything. ***The bible says "A righteous man may fall 7 times, he will rise again.*** The sun which always rise and shine every day may one day refused to shine due to the weather condition. Many people use to be the world richest beings on earth but now they are fallen because of minus mistake, some people wind had blown and the glory has departed. A lot of people have fallen because of many reasons. Some follow a wrong counsel with the hope that things will work out fine only to realize it went to unwanted areas. Sometime people fall a victim in the hand of greedy partner who dumped them and take away their money, which made things to fall apart and a strong man before now turn to a beggar. What a pity! There are many rich men of yesterday which had faded away. The mighty are really fallen.

I remember in United Kingdom and America when the economy fell due to September eleven story of the suicide bomber that blew the twin towers and the sudden collapse of Northern rock. All these incidents lead to the fall of many rich people. This is why you need to give to the fallen to help them to rise up. Anything you do in life is for your own benefit, never give up, you will soon receive the reward or better still you are reserving something for the sake of you generation to come "whatsoever you sow you shall reap if you faint not.

Please follow the logic of money and watch how money will flow into your life. Successful people on earth follow these rules and today they make it to the top. You can do the same; nothing is too difficult just one step at a time and trust God with the rest.

My prayer is that God will give you wisdom in all the areas of your life, to understand the logic of money, so that you will enter into the covenant of God's financial prosperity both now and forevermore in Jesus' name. Amen.

THE SUMMARY OF THE LOGIC OF MONEY

- BIG PEOPLE TALK ABOUT IDEAS, AVERAGE PEOPLE TALK ABOUT THINGS, SMALL PEOPLE TALK ABOUT OTHER PEOPLE.
1. **WORKING**. (INCOME) 2 THESS.3:10) NEVER STAY IDLE, BE A WORKING FORCE, BE DILIGENT IN WHAT YOU DO. WORK SMARTLY-NO WORKS, NO FOOD.
2. **SAVING** (BANKING SYSTEM) - *MATT 25:27* SAVING ACCOUNT, BUSINESS ACCOUNT, CURRENT ACCOUNT, ISA. FIXED DEPOSIT ACCOUNT. PARTNER OR CONTRIBUTION, SELF DISCIPLINE SAVING (CUP OF COFFEE) MONEY IS A SPIRIT AND MONEY CAN FLY AT ANY TIME.
3. **INVESTING**. (BUSINESS)- *MATT.25:14-18* START YOUR OWN BUSINESS (HAIRDRESSER, TAILOR, PLUMBER, TEACHER, CHILD MINDER...ETC) SELF EMPLOYMENT, PARTNERSHIP, LIMITED / UNLIMITED LAIBILITY. DEVELOP YOUR TALENT / SKILL.
- **TYPES OF INVESTMENTS**- LEVERAGE (**OPM**), PRECIOUS METAL, TREASURY BILLS, MONEY MARKET, STOCK & SHARES, BONDS, COMMODITIES, MARKET, RETIREMENT FUND, GENERAL BUSINESS,REAL ESTATE.
4. **SPENDING** (EXPENSES)- *LUKE 15:14* SPEND YOUR MONEY WISELY, TREAT YOURSELF UP TO YOUR WILDEST DREAM, ENJOY LIFE TO THE MAXIMAL LIVE COMFORTABLY. *LIFE IS TOO SHORT AFTER ALL IT'S YOUR MONEY.*
5. **GIVING**. (SOWING) *LUKE.6:38* DO NOT BE GREEDY PAY YOUR TITHE, OFFERING, ALMS TO THE POOR, CHARITY, BUY GIFTS TO PEOPLE, SEND MONEY TO YOUR PARENTS. BLESS YOUR MENTOR WHO SOWS SEEDS OF GREATNESS INTO YOUR LIFE (REMEMBER THE FAIR, THE FAITHFUL, THE FORTRESS, THE FALLEN)

CHAPTER TEN
THE FIVE RULES OF LAW IN MONEY

There is some magic in wealth, which can thus make a person pay their court to it, when it does not even benefit them. How strange it is, that a fool or knave, with riches, should be treated with more respect by the world, than a good man, or a wise man in poverty! Ann Radclife

By now, I hope you have gained something out of the information from the beginning of the book to this current page. Success is not a destiny but a journey. What you have learned in this book is not what matters but what you will make use of. Wrapping up in this chapter, I'd like you to know that we both have a part to play to arrive at our destination. Both the poor and the rich in our society have one thing in common: everybody is born the same. Although the sex may be different, both are given the same head and brain alike, eyes to see, ears for hearing, mouth to speak, and the heart to live. We all have emotions, feelings, and attitudes. Some may be born white or black, but all people throughout the globe have same body features.

For your information, everybody got access to 24 hours in a day. Individuals have power to make their choices. Our universe is guided by rules which enable us to function effectively. **Without rules things will fall apart and the centre will be disastrous**. Orderliness can only be guaranteed where rules are in place and even animals also abide by these rules.

Let us take a look at some of these rules in life which I will encourage you to pay close attention to because they are some of the most important parts of our life if you want to make money or be successful in this life.

(1) THE RULE OF CHOICE

The late Bob Marley's song says "Everybody gets the right to decide his own destiny". In another words, you have the power to choose what you want to be in life. You can decide to be poor or rich, the choices are yours. In my choice as the author of this book, I have poured out all available information in my life into this book with the hope that you will take a step and be what God created you to be in this world. It is your own choice to determine what you'd like to do with this book. Some may even be glancing through and in spite of my knowledge be thinking *"This book look like one of the books I have read"*. The choice is yours; you have the right to choose what you want to do.

The desire of every parent is for their children to grow up and become great in life, which is the reason why most parents will go many miles to educate their children and train them for the benefit of their future. But are all children well-trained? Or educated? That is another power of choice.

According to the Bible, God gave Adam the power of choice between the eating of all the available fruits and the forbidden fruit which was located in the centre of the Garden of Eden. Adam decided to eat the forbidden fruit and therefore introduced human beings to sickness and today we are subject to death due to Adam's choice. My point is that even though you may have the right to the rule of choice, there are always consequences toward every choice, either good or bad. Reading many books on success does not warrant you to be successful. You may be taught by any of the greatest teachers that ever lived, yet this does not grant you knowledge. In the science of life, age is a number. What counts are years of achievement. Jesus Christ died at the age of 33 years yet he impacted our generation with great secrets of blessing more than Methuselah who lives 969 years on earth. The choice is yours. You've chosen to buy and devote your time to reading this book (my appreciation if someone gave you this book as a gift but please, order your own copy, either to keep or also be a blessing.) *Be careful to make the right choices as your future of achievement will also be determined by your present choices.*

(2) THE RULE OF TIME

Many times people say "I don't have time." and you will be wondering what on Earth are they talking about because there are 24 hours which make a day. They may be correct in their own theory, but the truth of the matter is that either their own mind is lying to them or they have programmed the wrong philosophy to their own mind. When people say they have no time, what it actually meant is that they have no proper plan in place or balanced lifestyle in action. What you cannot achieve in daylight may be achieved in the night. It all depends on which angle you view things. The Bible says there is time for everything and season for every activity. ***Where discipline is in place, time can also be achieved.***

Most people waste their precious time with irrelevant circumstances. What you cannot derive with natural power could be achieved with few minutes of creative thinking and what you can obtain with step of action may be delayed if you spend all your life thinking. According to the rule of time in my own belief, everybody has equal time to spend in a day. This is a generous gift God has given to everybody in life. Time will help us to measure our progress, assist us to know when to start and when to stop; it will also help us to plan either to sleep or to awake. Time is very useful without the existence of time, it would be impossible for people to know when they are born and when they've died. Everything you see on this planet was achieved in the process of time, spiritually, materially, technologically.

Sometime ago it was impossible to communicate with our friends on the other side of town, but thank God for Face book with the help of internet and computers, people can now interact with one another at the click of a button.

Time is very precious especially if you want to acquire money. ***The time you waste will be the money you will never have.*** Many people think by delaying certain things they may have more in the future. It's never worked out like that. Whatever you're doing, do it in time, for time waits for no man. Nevertheless, everybody's got their own season. You only need to identify your own time and season. This is what I call the rule of time.

WHAT MAMA TOLD ME

When I was a young boy my mother told me something which I will always remember, she said there are people that will find it difficult to buy a car when it's cheaper in price, but can afford ten of the same cars when it's most expensive. Life is not about now only, it could also mean then. You may not be able to do certain things in a certain time- that doesn't qualify you to be a loser. Things may not have worked out for your interest in the past; you may even be in the midst of many opportunities and still no sign of achievement. Many of your friends may be doing well and yet you are still struggling, please never resign to failure. It's a matter of time. Some people's time may be now while others' are later; you only have to be sensitive to timing when it's time for you to shine. Please keep your star up high and shine like a star and if the cloud is still dark and there is no sign of rain please learn to wait for the right time as impatience is very dangerous.

(3) THE RULE OF IDENTIFICATION

One day, a man after spending much time with his close friends asked them a simple question "Who do people says I am? Surprisingly, they began to say all sort of thing and He further asked them saying "who do you think I am? Still most of the people were saying different things except one faithful among them who helped to identify.

The world is full of all kinds of people-too numerous to recognize and this is the main reason why everything must be labeled and given a name. Your identification will single you out in the crowd and make you to stand out. The more you know your identity the better you perform. Sadly though, most people do not recognize themselves and they live on earth as if they never existed at all. They never make any impact whatsoever. Being this type of person doesn't necessary mean they have not achieved anything in life, the problem is that their products have never been labeled or never identified due to carelessness. Some in the process of a quick fix have sold out their right and others have put all their great effort on their own label. Life can be funny. Sometimes people work so hard to get to where they are, and they have produced marvelous, incredible things that can acquire them money but due to foolishness, all their efforts will drop down under the carpet only for the wise to rebrand or package the same ideas in another label and start making money while the original owner ends up in poverty.

HUMILITY IS NOT HUMILIATION

Identification is very important, so you have to treasure it. Make it known everywhere you have the power to reach, Let people know your logo, and do not operate under secrecy. If you are laying foundations it's all right but afterwards, go public and let your identity be known. The Bible says no one lights the candle and puts it under the bed. You are a house built on top of the mountain, and you cannot be hiding. Humility is never humiliation. Some people pretend to be humble they have humiliated themselves. The future they plan for never comes to pass, their identity is being stolen away and they are living in confusion with the belief that God wants them to be like that. For your information, everything you see around you in this planet has never been identified by God the creator.

He gave us power to identify everything and whatever you call anything is what God knows it to be - ***Gen.2:19-20***.

You can identify what you want your life to be either poor or rich, slave or free, success or failure. You have the power to carry your identity everywhere you go. Every time people call you a name, it's the identity you have allowed yourself to carry and if you do not like what people call you, the right is in your hand to change and re-label yourself. ***The rule of identity says what so ever you wish to be called shall surely be what you are called***. If you give people your identity be expecting the announcement sooner or later.

YOU CAN HAVE A NEW IDENTITY

During secondary school, as a student of literature; I was given a story to read which had the word "PAAGA" (in my native language Yoruba it means suddenly) mistakenly I pronounced it two times and before I apologized the whole class had given me a new nickname a.k.a "DOUBLE PAAGA". I was so upset but the more I got angry the more my new name became popular and it was spreading like wildfire among the students. One day, a teacher called me and advised me what to do and as I followed the order, the name faded away and a new name emerged which I loved and by the time I got out of the school I got a new identity. What I am saying is, if you do not like what you are called for any reason, please get another identity and if you are finding it difficult due to any reason, why not allow God to help you? As recorded in the Bible "If a man is in Christ, behold old things are passed away and behold all things have become new".

Many people are enjoying a new identity from Jesus Christ. You too can do the same by giving your life to him.

(4) THE RULE OF UNSEEN FORCE

One faithful romantic evening, I took my sweetheart to a cinema to watch a very interesting movie titled Enemy *of the State*. It features Will Smith as the lead actor, in this movie, Robert Clayton Dean (Will Smith) is a lawyer with a wife and family whose happily normal life is turned upside down after a chance meeting with a college buddy lingerie shop. Unknown to the lawyer, he's just been burdened with a videotape of a congressman's assassination. Hot on the trail of this tape is a ruthless group of National Security Agents commanded by a belligerently ambitious Fed named Reynolds (Jon Vought). Using surveillance from satellites, bugs, and other sophisticated snooping devices, the NSA infiltrates every facet of Dean's existence, tracing each physical and digital footprint he leaves. Driven by acute paranoia, Dean enlists the help of a clandestine former NSA operative named Brill (Gene Hackman), and *Enemy of the State* kicks into high-intensity hyper drive. As I sat down inside the cinema gluing my eyes on the wide screen to catch every clip of this film, the spirit of the Lord Ministered to my heart by connecting me to the scripture Ephesians 6:12 ***"For our struggle is not against flesh and blood, but against the rulers, against the authorities, against the powers of this dark world and against the spiritual forces of evil in the heavenly realms."***

Unseen forces are wicked people who never want your progress in life. They operate in a secret ways especially in darkness. Their motive is to pursue, overtake and capture people's belongings. This is warfare. Unseen forces will terrorize people future with all power, and paralyze all their efforts. They operate in styles and fashions that never can be understood by any great philosophy in life, and their mission is to kill, steal, and destroy. (John 10:10) If an enemy attacks you, probably you can call for backup (police force). Unseen forces do not usually fight a physical battle but in a hideout such as in a dream of the night and they come deceiving, they appear to be friends who have your trust and you will never imagine such atrocity from this kind of people.

Most people are very ignorant about unseen forces, which I call a spiritual battle. Whenever things are to work out for their interest, something just happens, especially when a good thing is about to surface and all they see is failure all around. They have worked very hard to achieve a desirable success only to find out things never work out. Where others are making waves, they tread the same root only to be met with defeat, hardship, and frustration. All these are signs of unseen forces, the rule of unseen forces says ***as long as you're unable to identify the forces behind your downfall, they are powerful enough to destroy everything without apology***.

Unseen forces are operating in all categories of life. Either you believe it or not, Ignorance is never an excuse before the rules of law. If you never experience uncomfortable situations about your success, please do not pretend as if you lack the understanding of spiritual things. although you may not know what to do, seek advice from those who know about spiritual things and you will be amazed at the result! After all, when you perceive sickness, you seek doctor's assistance.

(5) THE RULE OF KNOWLEDGE

Knowledge is power. The more you know, the better you become in life. Ignorance is darkness while knowledge is light. When God created the world, He hid everything under the soil and bush. Only the man of understanding will be able to coordinate the raw material and develop them to human usage. It takes knowledge for Wright brothers to develop the aircraft we fly on the sky today. Imagine if there are no airplanes. We could have still been riding on the horses to travel across the Atlantic Ocean. Knowledge produces all the benefits of life. Whatever that exists on Earth today is as a result of knowledge. Where there is no knowledge, all things stand still.

The rule of knowledge says make use of what you know to get what you lack and it's only come as a result of intensive study. The more you study the better you have great understanding; stop learning and your power of knowledge will stop. The rule also says what so ever you know put them to practice and study more. God gave us a brain to store information and apply it where applicable. Money can only come from the new information you have and others don't have a clue. After the arrival of the internet on the computer, many people started developing their own knowledge of what to do with this latest technology. Face book came with a fresh knowledge of how to use pictures to connect with families and friends; right now they are making billions of dollars. If you can still remember. My Space was also there for a long time including many other friendly social connections on the internet, but out of the blue, Face book came with the ideas of sending pictures rather than just chatting and messaging. Right now they are making waves Years back, if you are travelling as a driver you need to have an Atlas Map to assist you on a journey, and if you didn't know how to read a map you may end up delaying the journey which can result into big headache.

USE YOUR NAVIGATOR

Presently, the use of maps has become old fashioned with the arrival of the navigator which is more of convenient to use as a driver. You only have to program the system and drive until a voice announces "you have arrived at your destination".

Knowledge will grant you access to money making as long as you follow the rules. Everybody has the right to knowledge of any kind in this world. **2 Timothy 2:15** says *"Study yourself to be approving workmanship that isn't ashamed but rightly divides the word of truth."*

Never stop learning, read books, search the internet, go back to school, have a listening ear, connect to people of understanding, ask questions, study your environment to know what problem you can fix. All these are the rules of knowledge which allows you to acquire money, please never go to school to study a subject because everybody are doing the same in fact this is a mistake of application knowledge. Use your own initiative and study what others do not have the knowledge of. That is where money lies. See what you can do when others are giving up on what they consider impossible; this is the secret of money making.

THERE IS HOPE

Years of much studying doesn't guarantee you success. What gives you success is the ability to make use of what you know right in time. As you begin to understand these principals you will start to experience the great power of money making. Never underestimate what your knowledge could give to you-put it to action and see the exceptional glory.

Let me finish by sharing a story of a man who after arriving in Europe couldn't make it for many years of unfruitful efforts. He decided to go back to his native land. Upon his arrival, the man went to the village to visit his grandfather who noticed bumps on the man's head. There was a simple quick solution. The man was very surprised to know that such a solution could exist for the treatment of bumps so easily where as in Europe a lot of people are suffering from the same similar problem. After few lessons from his grandfather the man travelled back abroad and applied his new knowledge by rendering service to people with similar problems and within a few months the man acquired great money.

You too can make money out of your dream if you make use of uncommon knowledge. Whatever you are going through now can become the experiences that will eventually lead to your success.

CONCLUSION

I hope by now you have been impacted by all the knowledge you have come across in this book. Please, I do not want you to read this book and quickly forget all about the principles. All the information are heavenly inspired and the majority of the stories are all true life stories either directly related or some are what I have read personally in the books written by successful authors. These have inspired me in all aspects of life coming from secular leaders, spiritual leaders, students, teachers, lay men, children or parents.

Life is not about how long you live but the impact you make. Just like money, it's not how much you know about it, rather it's how much you've acquired and what you do with money also matter.

YOUR TIME HAS COME

Many times in life, some people have tried everything, read all kinds of books still everything could not work out as expected. Please never give up and do not take alternative routes for an answer. The problem of life is that most people compare themselves with others; this is why people get things wrong and live a frustrated life. The will of God for individuals as Christians is different. That is why you need to wait upon the Lord.

He will renew your strength. God has not forgotten anyone, like I said before it's a matter of time. Life can be likened to a garden where you have all sorts of crops, such as vegetables, potatoes, corn, tomatoes, apples, cotton, etc. Out of these listed crops take tomatoes for instance, it will grow in a maximum of three months. Corn needs six months before its harvested. All the while, apples may not be able to grow quickly from the soil and when the apple harvest time arrives you cannot compare the profit with others, likewise cotton and other crops.

GUIDE YOUR HEART

Success always comes in many packages, if you ever want to be successful you need to go through tough situations and learn different kinds of lessons. Each time you pass through the channel of challenges, sometimes it will seem like you should quit, please its part of the game, stick your mind to what you believe, it will surely come to pass.

God is about to change things around his children and I want you to be sensitive in your spirit. As I conclude this book, follow all the guidance, and above all please if you have not sown into people's lives, start immediately. If you don't know who to send your seed to, you may as well sow into my own life by sending it to my mailing address with your special prayer request or testimony.

Lastly, may I advise you to never joke with the issue of tithing in your congregation as God promises open the window of heaven for your sake and all these promises can only develop from your heart. Nevertheless, learn how to renew your mind and guide your heart strongly for the perfect will of God to be accomplished in your life as recorded in the Bible. **Proverbs 4:23** *"Keep your heart with all diligence, for out of it springs the issues of life".*

Now that you have learnt the secret of acquiring money be expectant because *Money only comes to those who are expecting it.*

THE SUMMARY OF THE RULE
OF LAW IN MONEY

- *Without rules things will fall apart and the centre will be disastrous.*

(1) THE RULE OF CHOICE
- *Be careful to make the right choices as your future of achievement will also be determined by your present choices.*

(2) THE RULE OF TIME
- *Where discipline is in place, time can also be achieved.*
- *The time you waste will be the money you will never have*

(3) THE RULE OF IDENTIFICATION
- *The rule of identity says what so ever you wish to be called shall surely be what you are called*

(4) THE RULE OF UNSEEN FORCE
- *As long as you're unable to identify the forces behind your downfall, they are powerful enough to destroy everything without apology.*

(5) THE RULE OF KNOWLEDGE
- *Keep your heart with all diligence, for out of it springs the issues of life".*
- *Money only comes to those who are expecting it.*

APPRENDIX
MONEY RELATED BIBLE VERSES.

1. **Hebrews 13:5** "Keep your life free from love of money, and be content with what you have, for He has said, "I will never leave you nor forsake you."
2. **1 Timothy 6:10** "For the love of money is a root of all kinds of evils. It is through this craving that some have wandered away from the faith and pierced themselves with many pangs.
3. **Luke 16:11** "If then you have not been faithful in the unrighteous wealth, who will entrust to you the true riches?
4. **Jeremiah 32:9** "And I bought the field at Anathoth from Hanamel my cousin, and weighed out the money to him, seventeen shekels of silver.
5. **Matthew 6:24** "No one can serve two masters, for either he will hate the one and love the other, or he will be devoted to the one and despise the other. You cannot serve God and money.
6. **Jeremiah 32:10** "I signed the deed, sealed it, got witnesses, and weighed the money on scales."
7. **Proverbs 22:7** " The rich rule over the poor, and the borrower is the slave of the lender."
8. **Luke 19:23** "Why then did you not put my money in the bank, and at my coming? I
   might have collected it with interest?'
9. **Luke 14:28** "For which of you, desiring to build a tower, does not first sit down and count the cost, whether he has enough to complete it?
10. **Proverbs 21:20** "Precious treasure and oil are in a wise man's dwelling, but a foolish man devours it."
11. **Proverbs 1 3:22** "A good man leaves an inheritance to his children's children, but the sinner's wealth is laid up for the righteous."
12. **2 Kings 12:4** "Jehoash said to the priests, "All the money of the holy things that is brought into the house of the Lord, the money

for which each man is assessed the money from the assessment of persons and the money that a man's heart prompts him to bring into the house of the Lord,

13. **1 Peter 1:18** "Knowing that you were ransomed from the futile ways inherited from your forefathers, not with perishable things such as silver or gold,"

14. **Acts 20:33** I coveted no one's silver or gold or apparel.

15. ***Acts 8:20*** "But Peter said to him, "May your silver perish with you, because you thought you could obtain the gift of God with money!"

16. ***Acts 3:6*** "But Peter said, "I have no silver and gold, but what I do have I give to you. In the name of Jesus Christ of Nazareth, rise up and walk!"

17. ***Luke 22:5*** "And they were glad, and agreed to give him money.

18. ***Luke 19:15*** "When he returned, having received the kingdom, he ordered these servants to whom he had given the money to be called to him, that he might know what they had gained by doing business.

19. ***Luke 9:3*** "And he said to them, "Take nothing for your journey, no staff, or bag, or bread, or money; and do not have two tunics.

20. ***Mark 14:11*** And when they heard it, they were glad and promised to give him money. And he sought an opportunity to betray him.

21. ***Mark 12:41*** And he sat down opposite the treasury and watched the people putting money into the offering box. Many rich people put in large sums.

22. **Matthew 27:3** When Judas, his betrayer, saw that Jesus was condemned, he changed his mind and brought back the thirty pieces of silver to the chief priests and the elders,

23. **Matthew 25:27** "Then you ought to have invested my money with the bankers, and at my coming I should have received what was my own with interest.

24. **Matthew 25:18** "But he who had received the one talent went and dug in the ground and hid his master's money.

25. **Matthew 22:21** "They said, "Caesar's." Then he said to them, "Therefore render to Caesar the things that are Caesar's, and to God the things that are God's."

26. **Matthew 22:20** "And Jesus said to them, "Whose likeness and inscription is this?"

27. **Matthew 10:9** "Acquire no gold nor silver nor copper for your belts,

28. **Matthew 6:31-33** "Therefore do not be anxious, saying, 'What shall we eat?' or 'What shall we drink?' or 'What shall we wear?' For the Gentiles seek after all these things and your heavenly Father know that you need them all. But seek first the kingdom of God and his righteousness, and all these things will be added to you."

29. **Matthew 6:19-21** "Do not lay up for yourselves treasures on earth, where moth and rust destroy and where thieves break in and steal, but lay up for yourselves treasures in heaven, where neither moth nor rust destroys and where thieves do not break in and steal. For where your treasure is, there your heart will be also.

30. **Matthew 2:11** And going into the house they saw the child with Mary his mother,
and they fell down and worshiped him. then, opening their treasures, they offered him gifts, gold and frankincense and myrrh.

31. **Zechariah 11:12** Then I said to them, "If it seems good to you, give me my wages;
but if not, keep them." And they weighed out as my wages thirty pieces of out as silver.

32. **Micah 3:11** "Its heads give judgment for a bribe; its priests teach for a price; its prophets practice divination for money; yet they lean on the Lord and say, "Is not the Lord in the midst of us? No disaster shall come upon us."

33. **Amos 8:5** Saying, "When will the new moon be over, that we may sell grain? And When the Sabbath, that we may offer wheat for sale, that we may make the ephah small and the shekel great and deal deceitfully with false balances.

34. **Ezekiel 28:4** By your wisdom and your understanding you have made wealth for yourself, and have gathered gold and silver into your treasuries;

35. **Ezekiel 7:19** "They cast their silver into the streets, and their gold is like an unclean thing. Their silver and gold are not able to deliver them in the day of the wrath of the Lord. They cannot satisfy their hunger or fill their stomachs with it. For it was the stumbling block of their iniquity.

36. **Jeremiah 32:44** Fields shall be bought for money, and deeds shall be signed and sealed and witnessed, in the land of Benjamin, in the

places about Jerusalem, and in the cities of Judah, in the cities of the hill country, in the cities of the Shephelah, and in the cities of the Negeb; for I will restore their fortunes, declares the Lord."

37. **Jeremiah 32:25** Yet you, O Lord God, have said to me, "Buy the field for money and get witnesses" though the city is given into the hands of the Chaldeans.'"

38. **Isaiah 60:9** For the coastlands shall hope for me, the ships of Tarshish first, to bring your children from afar, their silver and gold with them, for the name of the Lord your God, and for the Holy One of Israel, because he has made you beautiful.

39. **Isaiah 55:2** Why do you spend your money for that which is not bread and your labor for that which does not satisfy? Listen diligently to me, and eat what is good,
and delight yourselves in rich food.

40. **Isaiah 55:1** "Come, everyone who thirsts, come to the waters; and he who has no money, come, buy and eat! Come; buy without money and without price.

41. **Isaiah 52:3** For thus says the Lord: "You were sold for nothing, and you shall be redeemed without money."

42. **Isaiah 46:6** Those who lavish gold from the purse, and weigh out silver in the scales, hire a goldsmith, and he makes it into a god; then they fall down and worship!

43. **Isaiah 13:17** Behold, I am stirring up the Medes against them, who have no regard for silver and do not delight in gold.

44. **Ecclesiastes 10:19** Bread is made for laughter, and wine gladdens life, and money answers everything.

45. **Ecclesiastes 7:12** For the protection of wisdom is like the protection of money, and the advantage of knowledge is that wisdom preserves the life of him who has it.

46. **Proverbs 7:20** He took a bag of money with him; at full moon he will come home."

47. **Psalm 15:5** Who does not put out his money at interest and does not take a bribe against the innocent. He who does these things shall never be moved.

48. **Nehemiah 5:10** Moreover, I and my brothers and my servants are lending them money and grain. Let us abandon this exacting of interest.

49. **Nehemiah 5:4** And there were those who said, "We have borrowed money for the king's tax on our fields and our vineyards.

50. **Ezra 8:25-27** And I weighed out to them the silver and the gold and the vessels, the offering for the house of our God that the king and his counselors and his lords and all Israel their present had offered. I weighed out into their hand 650 talents of silver, and silver vessels worth 200 talents and 100 talents of gold, 20 bowls of gold worth 1,000 darics, and two vessels of fine bright bronze as precious as gold.

51. **Ezra 7:17** With this money, then, you shall with all diligence buy bulls, rams, and lambs, with their grain offerings and their drink offerings, and you shall offer them on the altar of the house of your God that is in Jerusalem.

52. **Ezra 3:7** So they gave money to the masons and the carpenters, and food, drink, and oil to the Sidonians and the Tyrians to bring cedar trees from Lebanon to the sea, to Joppa, according to the grant that they had from Cyrus, king of Persia.

53. **2 Chronicles 34:17** They have emptied out the money that was found in the house of the Lord and have given it into the hand of the overseers and the workmen.

54. **2 Chronicles 34:14** While they were bringing out the money that had been brought into the house of the Lord, Hilkiah the priest found the Book of the Law of the Lord given through Moses.

55. **2 Chronicles 34:9** They came to Hilkiah the high priest and gave him the money that had been brought into the house of God, which the Levites, the keepers of the threshold, had collected from Manasseh and Ephraim and from all the remnant of Israel and from all Judah and Benjamin and from the inhabitants of Jerusalem.

56. **2 Chronicles 24:14** And when they had finished, they brought the rest of the money before the king and Jehoiada, and with it were made utensils for the house of the
Lord, both for the service and for the burnt offerings, and dishes for incense and vessels of gold and silver. And they offered burnt offerings in the house of the
Lord regularly all the days of Jehoiada.

57. **2 Chronicles 24:11** "And whenever the chest was brought to the king's officers by the Levites, when they saw that there was much money in it, the king's secretary and the officer of the chief priest would come and empty the chest and take it and return it

to its place. thus they did day after day, and collected money in abundance.

58. **2 Chronicles 24:5** And he gathered the priests and the Levites and said to them, "Go out to the cities of Judah and gather from all Israel money to repair the house of your God from year to year, and see that you act quickly." But at the Levites did not act quickly.

59. **1 Chronicles 21:25** So David paid Ornan 600 shekels of gold by weight for the site.

60. **2 Kings 23:35** And Jehoiakim gave the silver and the gold to Pharaoh, but he taxed the land to give the money according to the command of Pharaoh. He exacted the silver and the gold off the people of the land, from everyone according to his assessment, to give it to Pharaoh Neco.

61. **2 Kings 22:9** And Shaphan the secretary came to the king, and reported to the king, "Your servants have emptied out the money that was found in the house and have delivered it into the hand of the workmen who have the oversight into of the house of the Lord."

62. **2 Kings 22:7** But no accounting shall be asked from them for the money that is delivered into their hand, for they deal honestly."

63. **2 Kings 15:20** Menahem exacted the money from Israel, that is, from all the wealthy men, fifty shekels of silver from every man, to give to the king of Assyria. So the king of Assyria turned back and did not stay there in the land.

64. **2 Kings 12:16** The money from the guilt offerings and the money from the sin offerings was not brought into the house of the Lord; it belonged to the priests.

65. **2 Kings 12:7-16** Therefore King Jehoash summoned Jehoiada the priest and the other priests and said to them, "Why are you not repairing the house? Now therefore take no more money from your donors, but hand it over for the repair of the house." So the priests agreed that they should take no more money from the people, and that they should not repair the house. then Jehoiada the priest took a chest and bored a hole in the lid of it and set it beside the altar on the right side as one entered the house of the Lord. And the priests who guarded the threshold put in it all the money that was brought into the house of the Lord. And whenever they saw that there was much money in the chest, the king's secretary and

the high priest came up and they bagged and counted the money that was found in the house of the Lord. Then they would give the money that was weighed out into the hands of the workmen who had the oversight of the house of the Lord. And they paid it out to the carpenters and the builders who worked on the house of the Lord

66. **2 Kings 5:26** But he said to him, "Did not my heart go when the man turned from his chariot to meet you? Was it a time to accept money and garments, me to olive orchards and vineyards, sheep and oxen, male servants and female servants?

67. **1 Kings 21:15** As soon as Jezebel heard that Naboth had been stoned and was dead, Jezebel said to Ahab, "Arise, rise, take possession of the vineyard of Naboth the Jezreelite, which he refused to give you for money, for Naboth is not alive, but dead." And he said to her, "Because I spoke to Naboth the Jezreelite and said to him, 'Give me your vineyard for money, or else, if it pleases you, I will give you another vineyard for it.' And he answered, 'I will not give you my vineyard.

68. **1 Kings 21:2** And after this Ahab said to Naboth, "Give me your vineyard that I may have it for a vegetable garden, because it is near my house, and I will give you a better vineyard for it; or, if it seems good to you, I will give you its value in money."

69. **Judges 17:4** So when he restored the money to his mother, his mother took 200 pieces of silver and gave it to the silversmith, who made it into a carved image and a metal image. And it was in the house of Micah.

70. **Judges 17:2** And he said to his mother, "the 1,100 pieces of silver that were taken from you, about which you uttered a curse, and also spoke it in my ears, behold, the silver is with me; I took it." And his mother said, "Blessed be my son by the Lord."

71. **Judges 16:18** When Delilah saw that he had told her all his heart, she sent and called the lords of the Philistines, saying, "Come up again, for he has told me all his heart." then the lords of the Philistines came up to her and brought the money in their hands.

72. **Numbers 3:48-51** And give the money to Aaron and his sons as the redemption price for those who are over." So Moses took the redemption money from those who were over and above those redeemed by the Levites. From the firstborn of the people of Israel

he took the money, 1,365 shekels, by the shekel of the sanctuary. And Moses gave the redemption money to Aaron and his sons, according to the word of the Lord, as the Lord commanded Moses.

73. **Leviticus 27:18** But if he dedicates his field after the jubilee, then the priest shall he calculate the price according to the years that remain until the year of jubilee,
and a deduction shall be made from the valuation.

74. **Leviticus 27:15** And if the donor wishes to redeem his house, he shall add a fifth to the valuation price, and it shall be his.

75. **Leviticus 25:51** If there are still many years left, he shall pay proportionately for his redemption some of his sale price.

76. **Leviticus 25:37** You shall not lend him your money at interest, nor give him your food for profit.

77. **Leviticus 22:11** But if a priest buys a slave as his property for money, the slave may eat of it, and anyone born in his house may eat of his food.

78. **Leviticus 5:16** He shall also make restitution for what he has done amiss in the holy Thing and shall add a fifth to it and give it to the priest. And the priest shall make atonement for him with the ram of the guilt offering, and he shall be forgiven.

79. **Exodus 30:16** You shall take the atonement money from the people of Israel and shall give it for the service of the tent of meeting that it may bring the people of Israel to remembrance before the Lord, so as to make atonement for your lives."

80. **Exodus 22:25** "If you lend money to any of my people with you who are poor, you people shall not be like a moneylender to him, and you shall not exact interest from him.

81. **Exodus 22:17** If her father utterly refuse to give her to him, he shall pay money equal to the bride-price for virgins.

82. **Exodus 22:7** "If a man gives to his neighbor money or goods to keep safe, and it is stolen from the man's house, then, if the thief is found, he shall pay double.

83. **Exodus 21:34** The owner of the pit shall make restoration. He shall give money to its owner, and the dead beast shall be his.

84. **Exodus 21:11** And if he does not do these three things for her, she shall go out for nothing, without payment of money.

85. **Exodus 12:44** But every slave that is bought for money may eat of it after you have circumcised him.

86. **Genesis 47:14-18** And Joseph gathered up all the money that was found in the land of Egypt and in the land of Canaan, in exchange for the grain that they bought. And Joseph brought the money into Pharaoh's house. And when the money was all spent in the land of Egypt and in the land of Canaan, all the Egyptians came to Joseph and said, "Give us food. Why should we die before your eyes? For our money is gone." And Joseph answered, "Give your livestock, and I will give you food in exchange for your livestock, if your money is gone." So they brought their livestock to Joseph, and Joseph gave them food in exchange for the horses, the flocks, the herds, and the donkeys. He supplied them with food in exchange for all their livestock that year. And when that year was ended, they came to him the following year and said to him, "We will not hide from my lord that our money is all spent. The herds of livestock are my lord's. There is nothing left in the sight of my lord but our bodies and our land.

87. **Genesis 44:8** Behold the money that we found in the mouths of our sacks we brought back to you from the land of Canaan. How then could we steal silver or gold from your lord's house?

88. **Genesis 44:1-8** Then he commanded the steward of his house, "Fill the men's sacks with food, as much as they can carry, and put each man's money in the mouth of his sack, and put my cup, the silver cup, in the mouth of the sack of the youngest, with his money for the grain." And he did as Joseph told him. As soon as the morning was light, the men were sent away with their donkeys. They had gone only a short distance from the city. Now Joseph said to his steward, "Up, follow after the men, and when you overtake them, say to them, 'Why have you repaid evil for good? Is it not from this With that my lord drinks, and by this that he practices divination? You have done evil in doing this.

89. **Genesis 43:21** And when we came to the lodging place we opened our sacks, and there was each man's money in the mouth of his sack, our money in full weight. So we have brought it again with us,

90. **Genesis 43:12-23** Take double the money with you. Carry back with you the money that was returned in the mouth of your sacks. Perhaps it was an oversight. Take also your brother, and arise, go again to the man. May God Almighty grant you before the man, and may he send back your other brother and Benjamin. And

as for me, if I am bereaved of my children, I am bereaved." So the men took this present, and they took double the money with them, and Benjamin. They arose and went down to Egypt and stood before Joseph. When Joseph saw Benjamin with them, he said to the steward of his house, "Bring the men into the house, and slaughter an animal and make ready, for the men are to dine with me at noon.

91. **Genesis 42:25-35** And Joseph gave orders to fill their bags with grain, and to replace every man's money in his sack, and to give them provisions for the journey. This was done for them. then they loaded their donkeys with their grain and departed. And as one of them opened his sack to give his donkey fodder at the lodging place, he saw his money in the mouth of his sack. He said to his brothers, "My money has been put back; here it is in the mouth of my sack!" At this their hearts failed them, and they turned trembling to one another, saying, "What is this that God has done to us?" When they came to Jacob their father in the land of Canaan, they told him all that had happened to them, saying,

92. **Genesis 31:15** Are we not regarded by him as foreigners? For he has sold us, and he has indeed devoured our money.

93. **Genesis 24:35** The Lord has greatly blessed my master, and he has become great. He has given him flocks and herds, silver and gold, male servants and female servants,
camels and donkeys.

94. **Genesis 23:16** Abraham listened to Ephron, and Abraham weighed out for Ephron the silver that he had named in the hearing of the Hittites, four hundred shekels of silver, according to the weights current among the merchants.

95. **Genesis 2323:13** And he said to Ephron in the hearing of the people of the land, "But if you will, hear me: I give the price of the field. Accept it from me, that I may bury my dead there."

96. **Genesis 23:9** That he may give me the cave of Machpelah, which he owns; it is at the end of his field. For the full price let him give it to me in your presence as property for a burying place.

97. **Genesis 20:16** To Sarah he said, "Behold, I have given your brother a thousand pieces of silver. It is a sign of your innocence in the eyes of all who are with you, and before everyone you are vindicated."

98. **Genesis 17:27** And all the men of his house, those born in the house and those bought with money from a foreigner, were circumcised with him.

99. **Genesis 17:23** Then Abraham took Ishmael his son and all those born in his house or bought with his money, every male among the men of Abraham's house, and he circumcised the flesh of their foreskins that very day, as God had said to him.

100. **Genesis 13:2** Now Abram was very rich in livestock, in silver, and in gold.

101. **Luke 16:19-31** "There was a rich man who was clothed in purple and fine linen and who feasted sumptuously every day. And at his gate was laid a poor man named Lazarus, covered with sores, who desired to be fed with what fell from the rich man's table. Moreover, even the dogs came and licked his sores. The poor man died and was carried by the angels to Abraham's side. The rich man also died and was buried, in Hades, being in torment, he lifted up his eyes and saw Abraham far of and Lazarus at his side.

102. **Luke 16:13** No servant can serve two masters, for either he will hate the one and love the other, or he will be de voted to the one and despise the other. You cannot serve God and money."

103. **Mark 6:8** "He charged them to take nothing for their journey except a staff no bread, no bag, no money in their belts—

104. **Matthew 28:15** "So they took the money and did as they were directed. And this story has been spread among the Jews to this day.

105. **Matthew 28:12** And when they had assembled with the elders and taken counsel, they gave a sufficient sum of money to the soldiers

106. **Ecclesiastes 5:10** "He who loves money will not be satisfied with money, nor he who loves wealth with his income; this also is vanity.

107. **Proverbs 30:8-9** "Remove far from me falsehood and lying; give me neither poverty nor riches; feed me with the food that is needful for me, lest I be full and deny you and say, "Who is the Lord?" or lest I be poor and steal and profane the name of my God.

108. **Proverbs 23:4-5** Do not toil to acquire wealth; be discerning enough to desist. When your eyes light on it, it is gone, for suddenly it sprouts wings, flying like an eagle toward heaven.
109. **Proverbs 13:11** "Wealth gained hastily will dwindle, but whoever gathers little by little will increase it.

MONEY QUOTATION

1. Too many of us look upon Americans as dollar chasers. This is a cruel libel, even if it is reiterated thoughtlessly by the Americans themselves. **Albert Einstein (1879 - 1955)**
2. Poverty cannot deprive us of many consolations. It cannot rob us of the affection we have for each other, or degrade in our own opinion, of in that of any person, whose opinion we ought to value. **Ann Radcliffe**
3. There is some magic in wealth, which can thus make persons pay their court to it, when it does not even benefit them. How strange it is, that a fool or knave, with riches, should be treated with more respect by the world, than a good man, or a wise man in poverty! **Ann Radcliffe**
4. I feel good about taking things to Goodwill and actually, I do like shopping at Goodwill. It's so cheap that it feels like a library where I am just checking things out for a while until I decide to take them back.
5. He that is of the opinion money will do everything may well be suspected of doing everything for money. **Benjamin Franklin (1706 - 1790)**
6. If you would be wealthy, think of saving as well as getting.
7. Who is rich? He that is content. Who is that? Nobody.
8. Riches may enable us to confer favors', but to confer them with propriety and grace requires something that riches cannot give. **Charles Caleb Colton (1780 - 1832),**
9. Annual income twenty pounds, annual expenditure nineteen six, result: Happiness. Annual income twenty pounds, annual expenditure twenty pounds ought and six, result: Misery. **Charles Dickens (1812 - 1870)**
10. If all the rich people in the world divided up their money among themselves there wouldn't be enough to go around. **Christina Stead (1903 - 1983)**

11. Endless money forms the sinews of war. **Cicero (106 BC - 43 BC)**

12. If you want to know what God thinks of money, look at the people He gives it to **Donald Trump (1946)** *"Trump: Art of the Deal*

13. Money was never a big motivation for me, except as a way to keep score. The real excitement is playing the game. **Dr. Thomas Fuller (1654 - 1734)**

14. Money is the sinew of love as well as war. **E.E Cummings (1894 - 1962)**

15. I'm living so far beyond my income that we may almost be said to be living apart. **Edith Wharton (1862 - 1937)**

16. The only way not to think about money is to have a great deal of it.

17. Save a little money each month and at the end of the year you'll be surprised at how little you have. **Ernest Haskins**

18. My problem lies in reconciling my gross habits with my net income. **Errol Flynn**

19. The mint makes it first, it is up to you to make it last. **Evan Esar (1899 - 1995)**

20. The rich are the scum of the earth in every country. **G. K. Chesterton (1874 - 1936)**

21. Lack of money is the root of all evil. **George Bernard Shaw (1856 - 1950)**

22. One must be poor to know the luxury of giving. **George Eliot (1819 - 1880)**

23. Money frees you from doing things you dislike. Since I dislike doing nearly everything, money is handy. **Groucho Marx (1890 - 1977)**

24. The chief value of money lies in the fact that one lives in a world in which it is overestimated. **H. L. Mencken (1880 - 1956)**

25. Make money your god and it will plague you like the devil. **Henry Fielding (1707 - 1754)**

26. Make money, by fair means if you can, if not, by any means make money.

27. If you can count your money you don't have a billion dollars. **J. Paul Getty (1892 - 1976)**

28. I have enough money to last me the rest of my life, unless I buy something. **Jackie Mason (1934)**

29. A large income is the best recipe for happiness I ever heard of. **Jane Austen (1775 - 1817)**, *Mansfield Park*

30. A wise man should have money in his head, but not in his heart. **Jonathan Swift (1667 - 1745)**

31. Do not be fooled into believing that because a man is rich he is necessarily smart. There is ample proof to the contrary. **Julius Rosenwald (1862 - 1932)**

32. Be rich to yourself and poor to your friends **Juvenal (55 AD - 127 AD)**

33. It is not easy for men to rise whose qualities are thwarted by poverty. **Juvenal (55 AD - 127 AD)**, *Satires*

34. The easiest way for your children to learn about money is for you not to have any. **Katharine Whitehorn**

35. Lack of money is no obstacle. Lack of an idea is an obstacle. - **Ken Hakuta**

36. It is pretty hard to tell what does bring happiness; poverty and wealth have both failed. **Kin Hubbard (1868 - 1930)**

37. The safest way to double your money is to fold it over and put it in your pocket. - **Kin Hubbard (1868 - 1930)**

38. He had learned over the years that at poor people did not feel so poor when allowed to give occasionally. *Lawana Blackwell, Courtship of the Vicar's Daughter, 1998*

39. Money can't buy happiness, but neither can poverty. **Leo Rosten (1908)**

40. It is the wretchedness of being rich that you have to live with rich people. **Logan Pearsall Smith (1865 - 1946)**

41. You don't have to die in order to make a living. **Lynn Johnston (1947)**

42. Riches cover a multitude of woes. **Menander (342 BC - 292 BC)**, *Lady of Andros*

43. No matter how rich you become, how famous or powerful, when you die the size of your funeral will still pretty much depend on the weather. **Michael Pritchard**

44. The more you chase money, the harder it is to catch it. - **Mike Tatum**

45. It is better to have a permanent income than to be fascinating. **Oscar Wilde (1854 - 1900)**

46. Wealth is the parent of luxury and indolence, and poverty of meanness and viciousness, and both of discontent. **Plato (427 BC - 347 BC)**, *the Republic*
47. Money alone sets all the world in motion. **Publilius Syrus (~100 BC)**, *Maxims*
48. Money is the opposite of the weather. Nobody talks about it, but everybody does something about it. -**Rebecca Johnson**, *in 'Vogue'*
49. Someday I want to be rich. Some people get so rich they lose all respect for humanity. that's how rich I want n t to be. - **Rita Rudner**
50. Finance is the art of passing money from hand to hand until it finally disappears. **Robert W. Sarrnof W. Sa**
51. It has been said that the love of money is the root of all evil. Love of The want of money is so quite as truly. **Samuel Butler (1835 - 1902)**
52. Money's the same, whoever gives it to you. That was the point of money, after all: crisp and clean or wrinkled or disintegrated into quarters - a dollar was always worth a hundred cents. -**Scott Westerfelderfe**, *the Last Days, 2006*
53. A billion here, a billion there, pretty soon it adds up to real money. -**Senator Everett Dirksen (1896 - 1969)**
54. The art of living easily as to money is to pitch your scale of living one degree below your means. -**Sir Henry Taylor**
55. A little wanton money, which burned out the bottom of his purse. -**Sir Thomas More (1478 - 1535)**, *Works*
56. Money: there's nothing in the world so demoralizing as money. **Sophocles (496 BC - 406 BC)**, *Antigone*
57. Money can't buy friends, but it can get you a better class of enemy. **Spike Milligan**
58. I choose the likely man in preference to the rich man; I want a man without money rather than money without a man. -**Thomas Jefferson (1743 - 1826)**
59. Never spend your money before you have it. **W. Somerset Maugham (1874 - 1965)**
60. He had heard people speak contemptuously of money: he wondered if they had ever tried to do without it. **W. Somerset Maugham (1874- 1965)**,

61. Money is like a sixth sense without which you cannot make a complete use of the other five. -**W Somerset Maugham** *Edge,*
62. Perhaps the most important use of money - It saves time. Life is so short, and there's so much to do, one can't afford to waste a minute; and just think how much you waste. **William Cobbett (1763 - 1835)**
63. Be you in what line of life you may, it will be amongst of life your misfortunes if you have not time properly to attend to pecuniary [monetary]] matters. Want of attention to these matters has impeded the progress of science and of genius itself. -**William Jennings Bryan (1860 - 1925)**
64. No one can earn a million dollars honestly. **Woody Allen (1935-)**
65. Money is better than poverty, if only for financial reasons.

THE AUTHOR WANTS TO HEAR FROM YOU

PLEASE TELL ME HOW THIS BOOK "HOW TO ACQUIRE MONEY" HAS IMPACTED YOUR LIFE. I LOVE TO HEAR FROM YOU.

FOR MORE INFORMATION.

CONTACT:

PETER - OYEBOBOLA
0044(0)7961193137
Email:praisetek@hotmail.com
WEB SITE: www.praisetek.co.uk